MEMOIRS of
Lt. CAMILLO VIGLINO
Italian Air Force, 1915-1916

A First Hand Account
of the Earliest Days of
Military Aviation

Translated by his two children
Camilla Viglino Hurwitz and Victor Viglino

© Copyright 2001 Camilla Hurwitz. All rights reserved.

No part of this publication may be reproduced, stored in a retrieval system, or transmitted, in any form or by any means, electronic, mechanical, photocopying, recording, or otherwise, without the written prior permission of the copyright holder.

Front and back covers designed by Ragland Design, Park City, Utah.

Printed in Victoria, Canada

National Library of Canada Cataloguing in Publication Data

```
Viglino, Camillo, 1893-1935
 Memoirs of Lt. Camillo Viglino : Italian Air Force, 1915-1916
ISBN 1-55212-933-0
1. Viglino, Camillo, 1893-1935.
2. Italy.  Aeronautica--Biography.
3. World War, 1914-1918--Personal narratives, Italian.
I. Hurwitz, Camilla   II. Viglino, Victor    III. Title.
D640.V53 2001       940.4'4945         C2001-902600-5
```

TRAFFORD

This book was published *on-demand* **in cooperation with Trafford Publishing.**
On-demand publishing is a unique process and service of making a book available for retail sale to the public taking advantage of on-demand manufacturing and Internet marketing.
On-demand publishing includes promotions, retail sales, manufacturing, order fulfilment, accounting and collecting royalties on behalf of the author.

Suite 6E, 2333 Government St., Victoria, B.C. V8T 4P4, CANADA
Phone   250-383-6864   Toll-free   1-888-232-4444 (Canada & US)
Fax   250-383-6804   E-mail   sales@trafford.com
Web site   www.trafford.com   TRAFFORD PUBLISHING IS A DIVISION OF TRAFFORD HOLDINGS LTD.
Trafford Catalogue #01-0335   www.trafford.com/robots/01-0335.html

10   9   8   7   6   5   4   3   2

TRANSLATORS' ACKNOWLEDGEMENTS

To Dan Hurwitz, for his encouragement and for his contribution to the flow and the spirit of the English text.

To Camillo Viglino's three grandchildren, Paul Hurwitz, Karen Kurtin, and Mark Hurwitz for their constant support and for their many valuable suggestions which helped to shape the final document.

To Sid Hurwitz for his insightful critique and morale-boosting comments.

And to Fred Fischer and Wes Hahn who drew on their extensive aeronautical experience to graciously provide helpful technical advice.

Camilla Viglino Hurwitz
Victor Viglino

To my little son, Vittorio,
Whose generation will fly throughout the world.
In memory of the generation of his father
That dared the first timid flights.

Camillo Viglino
1934

Footnote: Viglino's second child, Camilla, was born six months after his death.

OFFICE OF THE GOVERNOR
TRIPOLI, LIBYA

June 22, 1934

Dear Mr. Viglino,

I have read your very informative book on the early days of aviation. It is interesting to note that the enthusiasm of the young men in those first flights has actually increased by a hundred fold today. The progress of the airplane has been greater than that of any other invention in the world. In fact, this century might appropriately be called "the century of aviation". The young pilots of today will be inspired by your book as they compare the modern art of flying with that of yesterday.

I forward my heartfelt thanks for your book and wish you the best of everything.

Italo Balbo
[Former Head of the Italian Air Force]

TABLE OF CONTENTS

PART I : THE WORLD WAR I YEARS

FOREWORD.. 3
THE FIRST LICENSE
   Malpensa Air Field..................................9
   First Flight...11
   Short Run... 13
   Long Run.. 15
   Tour of the Field.................................. 17
   Half Hour Flight................................... 21
   Final Tests for the First License......... 25
   Saint Elia's Intervention...................... 27
   Engineers Caproni and Pensuti........... 29
   Other Malpensa Adventures................ 31
THE SECOND LICENSE
   Busto Arsizio Air Field....................... 37
   Engines... 39
   Landing and Taking Off....................... 43
   Spiraling.. 47
   The Elements..................................... 49
   Other Busto Arsizio Adventures......... 57
   What We Wore to Fly......................... 61
   Final Tests for the Second License..... 67
   My Friends' Raids................................ 73
   Getting Lost....................................... 77
   My Raid... 79
CONCLUSION
   My Big Fall.. 89
   Flight of War...................................... 93
   Did I Ever Fly Again?.......................... 97

PART II : REFLECTIONS 20 YEARS LATER

FOREWORD... 103
AVIATION.. 105
THE AUTOMOBILE... 109
RADIO AND TELEVISION................................. 111
THE PHONOGRAPH... 113
THE BICYCLE.. 117
AFTERWORD.. 119

PART I: THE WORLD WAR I YEARS

FOREWORD

In July of 1915, just two months after Italy joined the Allied Forces during World War I, Lieutenant Camillo Viglino, age 23, volunteered for flight training in the Italian Air Force. Needless to say, his gallantry was strongly opposed by his patriarchal, upper-class family. Unfortunately, his career as a military pilot was a very brief one. Less than a year after his enlistment – on his first flight after having been awarded his Pilot's License – Viglino shattered his leg in a landing accident. His experiences in the air force were clearly recorded at the time they occurred and are diary-like in their form. The author's allusion to divine intervention in the daily lives of the young student pilots reflects his strong religious upbringing.

Although Viglino compiled his notes several years after his accident, his account retains the freshness and intimacy of an on-the-scene, first-hand report. The discomfort of flying an open-cockpit 1914 Maurice Farman, the frequent crashes at the flight school, and the difficulties of navigating in fog are all related with a nonchalant bravado befitting a twenty-year old. Viglino follows his diary-like entries with a copy of a letter from a cousin at the front describing an air raid on Adelsberg, Austria.

This book was written in Italian and originally published as "Venite a Volare Con Me" in 1934 by Societa Editrice Internazionale. It was translated into English by his two children, Camilla Viglino Hurwitz and Victor Viglino.

PREFACE

The full course for becoming a pilot during the war consisted of two parts. First we had to obtain the First License, which bestowed on us the title of *Cadet Pilot Aviator*. Upon completing the First License, we received the insignia of the Golden Eagles. Next we had to obtain the Second License, which bestowed on us the title of *Pilot Aviator*. Upon completing the Second License, we received the Royal Crown over our Golden Eagles.

I began my training for the First License at the Aviation Field of Malpensa toward the end of July, 1915. I began my training for the Second License at the Busto Arsizio Aviation Field in the middle of November, 1915 [see Figure 1].

These writings on my experiences were published for the first time in the magazine, "Review for the Young". It is my hope that they were enjoyed by young men when they first appeared in the magazine and that they will be enjoyed again in this book. I am dedicating this book to my little son, Vittorio, and to my little nephew, Silvio. I hope that when they grow up this book will help them to understand what flying was like for me many years earlier.

As I read this book today, the flying methods already seem primitive. Imagine what things will be like twenty or forty years from now. The airplane has just begun to have its impact on the world. Imagine how it will change the world when it becomes as established as the automobile and railroad.

Having experienced what flying was like with the first airplanes and seeing what flying is like with the airplanes of today, I have tried to look forward a little and predict what flying will be like several decades from now. These predictions are also included in this book.

I can't help but wonder if twenty or forty years from now people will still be interested in reading about what flying was like at the beginning of the war. If they are, I hope this book helps give them a vivid picture of the times.

Camillo Viglino
 1934

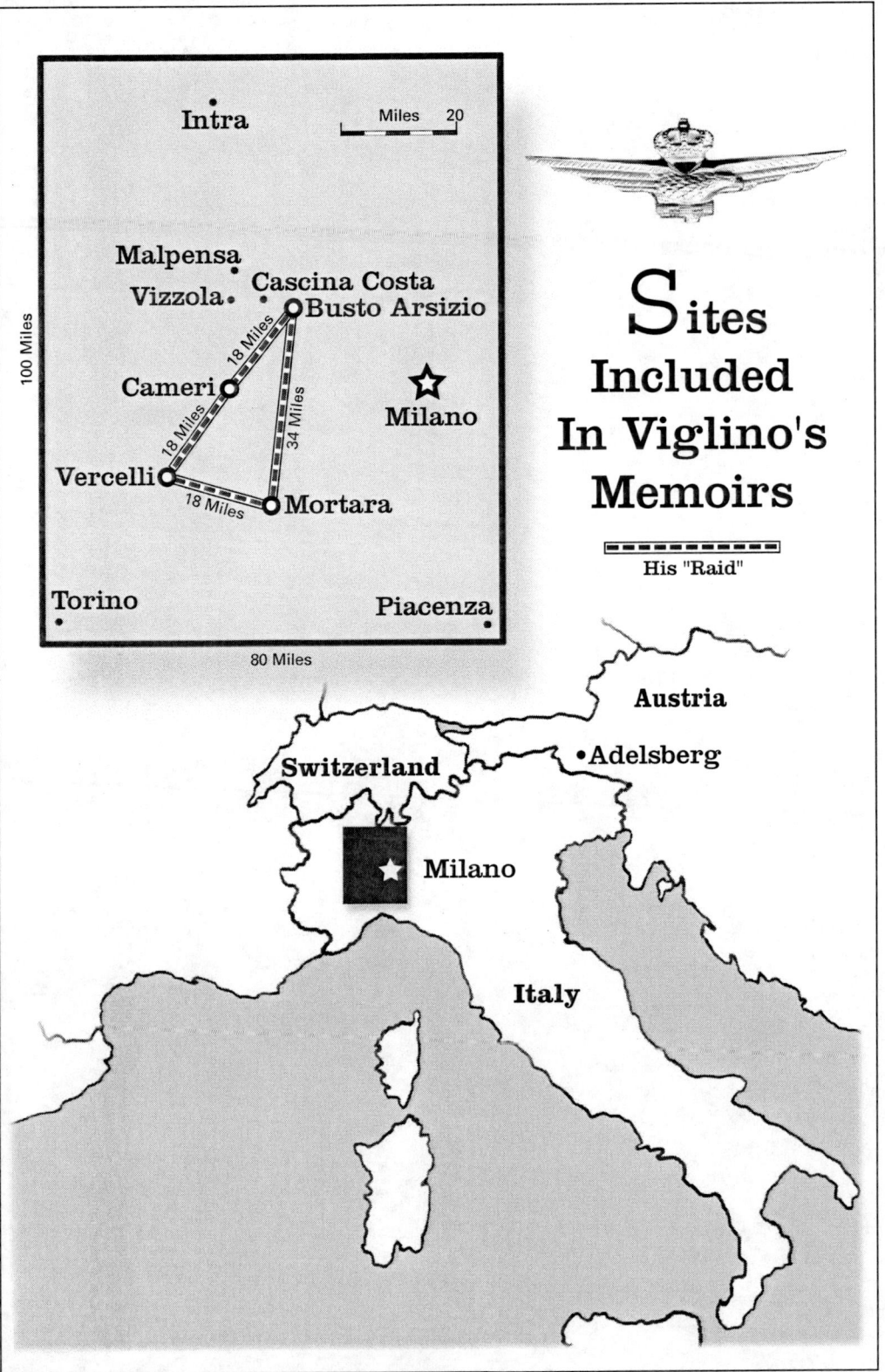

Figure 1

THE FIRST LICENSE

MALPENSA AIR FIELD

I began my training for the First License at the Malpensa Field near Somma Lombardo toward the end of July, 1915. At that time, heroics were an everyday part of aviation. That's why everyone stared in awe at the insignia of Golden Eagles imbedded on the shirt sleeve of those who had completed their First License. And just to make sure it was visible, it wasn't unusual to see a young pilot walking with his coat over his arm in the dead of winter. The risk of getting pneumonia seemed like a small price to pay for the admiration gained by the insignia. The pilot who succeeded in flying his plane over his own home town was written up in the local newspaper. In fact, every once in a while, a plane would disappear from the field for a time followed by an excited telephone call from the police of someone's home town thirty miles away informing us that the plane had been spotted overhead.

While we were working on our First License, we were called "Aspiring Pilot Aviators" and were given a metal propeller to wear on our hats. But of course, no "hazardous duty" pay to accompany it. To top it off, we had to contribute regularly to the purchase of funeral wreaths for our classmates killed in the training course. Once we completed the First License, we did receive a hazardous duty pay of about four liras per day. And after we completed the Second License, we received an additional hazardous duty pay of about three liras per day.

In those days only men from the engineering, artillery, and cavalry units were permitted to volunteer for pilot training. Ordinary infantrymen were not. Pilot trainees, such as myself, who generally came from upper class families, had therefore willingly left a relatively safe environment for one full of risk – the term "risk of luxury" was the way it was sometimes described.

At Malpensa, we flew the Maurice Farman, Model 1912 planes. The Model 1912 had the cockpit in front of the wings and the steering board, or as we called it, the stabilizer, in front of the cockpit. The plane was so easy to fly that in honor of the inventor, we named it "Maurizio: It will kill you only if you have a death wish". We also called it "Father of the Family" (see Figures 2 & 3).

Within a 100 square mile area of flat marshland there were four aviation fields – Busto Arsizio, Malpensa, and Cascina Costa for training the pilots, and Vizzola for testing the Caproni planes [see Figure 1]. The sky was therefore always full of airplanes crossing over and under each other in every which way. When the big Caproni bomber planes went by, the Farmans veered off and gave them the right of way out of respect.

Figure 2 – Maurice Farman Biplane, Model 1912. Note that the cockpit is in front of the wings and the stabilizer is in the front of the cockpit.

Figure 3 – The author and his Farman in 1915.

FIRST FLIGHT

At Malpensa there was a single road which, starting at the barracks, circled the field. Because it was the only road wide enough to accommodate the planes, it was also used as the runway and planes all lined up along it in preparation for take-off. Each plane was assigned to an instructor and a group of students. One by one they flew a few feet above the ground, ascending and descending in turn making very sure to stay on the road. The importance of staying on the road was to teach us precision landing and to avoid the damage to the plane and ourselves that could result from veering off the road. If you did veer off the road, you were suspended from flying for a day without flight pay.

First in line – farthest from the barracks – were the students who were making their first flight alongside an instructor. It was standard practice for the survivors of the "flight of terror" to pay for drinks all around immediately afterwards. First the student would fly as a passenger for about five minutes just to see if he could hack it. Often, he came back without having seen or understood anything because his goggles were never properly adjusted and the wind was so strong that he had to keep his eyes shut most of the time. If the first trip indicated that the student had what it took to fly, the training started. He and the instructor boarded a plane with dual controls. The instructor sat in front and handled the set of controls which could override those in the rear being used by the student. The student learned by imitating the actions of the instructor. The aviation lingo between them was full of idiomatic expressions created earlier by French pilots. These expressions included *taxi, take off, climb, dive, glide,* and *land.* Let's hope this foreign lingo will soon disappear.

When the instructor felt that the student was ready, he let him switch to the front controls and he would sit in the back correcting any mistakes the student was making. The controls were actually very intuitive and easily learned. A single lever was used for all directions. You pulled it towards you to climb, pushed it away from you to descend, tilted it left to roll to the left, and tilted it right to roll to the right. To conduct a full turn left or right, you simply stepped on the left or right pedal.

Unfortunately, not everything was easy. For example, it wasn't so easy to maintain the dynamic equilibrium of the plane, and without equilibrium, you quickly found yourself spiraling downwards like a falling leaf. Nor was it easy to determine from up high how to maneuver the plane so that you could land in a specific location. It wasn't so easy to land the plane upright at just the right time – a little too late and you slammed into the ground; a little too soon and the plane dropped downward from its own weight. In other words, you had to straighten the plane just as you touched the ground and at just the right speed to avoid nosing down or yawing. With all these problems, it wasn't at all unusual for us to end up slamming against houses or trees particularly if the landing area was unsuitable, which it often was.

SHORT RUN

After about twenty flights with the instructor, each lasting from five to ten minutes, we went on to the next exercise, called "taxiing". For taxiing we were alone in the plane and we stayed on the ground. The purpose of the exercise was to learn how to take off without yawing. If you weaved just a little, the plane could easily start to spin around itself and, at those take-off speeds, the carriage of the plane would detach and the plane would fall on its side, smashing against the ground.

Next we went on to the third exercise called the "Short Run". In the Short Run the student really flew alone for the first time. In this exercise, the student had to fly for a distance of about 300 feet, at about nine to twelve feet above the ground, and land. A classmate helped him turn the plane around at the end of each lap. On an average, a student would make anywhere from two to four Short Runs per day.

In the first few laps, the minimum damage was likely to be the breaking of the tension wires. There was one mechanic who was particularly good at repairing them and he would charge the students two cents per wire. From the sidelines the students urged him to hurry up complaining that they were wasting time that they wanted to spend making Short Runs.

What happened one day will help the reader understand the intensity of the mania which I had for flying. A burning plane fell quite close to me while I was in the process of practicing my Short Runs. Everyone else ran toward the plane. I, however, saw it as an opportunity to make more Short Runs than I would normally be able to make. Because even the classmate assigned to help me turn the plane around had run toward the burning plane, it took some heroic strength to turn the plane around by myself. Finally, I felt guilty for making Short Runs while others may have been dying – in fact, two men in the plane had been burned to death – and belatedly ran toward the wrecked plane.

The constant occurrence of disasters, and the knowledge that they could happen to you at any moment, left you feeling indifferent to the fate of others. When someone died or was injured, the authorities immediately removed him and quickly made us fly again so that we wouldn't have time to mull over the dangers.

On that particular evening, we all went to a small restaurant that we frequented often and ordered steak. Someone in our group noticed that the smell of the steaks resembled that of the charred bodies of the two men and he said so out loud. The rest of us just continued to eat our steak without comment. Today it happens to you; tomorrow it happens to me. It's all part of the game.

But don't think for a minute that we didn't have respect for our classmates killed in flight. When the field truck passed in front of the cemetery, we all saluted. And when we passed over the cemetery in flight, again we all saluted. We were saluting the friends that we could be joining at any moment. When we attended the funeral of our friends who died flying, the women would look at us all with eyes full of pity. But we were no more deserving of their pity than the infantrymen who died hungry, in dirty trenches filled with lice. I guess in contrast to them, we risked a cold death, often foreseen, all alone, without the excitement of the hand-to-hand combat to distract us from its approach.

LONG RUN

The Short Run taught us how to maintain a straight flight path and how to land. Next, we began practicing our fourth exercise, the "Long run". On the Long Run, we flew about 150 feet above the ground for a distance of about 1.5 miles. The Long Run made landing more difficult because at the higher altitude, we had to begin to deal with air turbulence. Standing on the ground, you can't imagine the vertical air currents which rise (updrafts) and descend (downdrafts) constantly even when the air is relatively calm. The ground, heated by the sun, warms the air immediately above it which, being lighter, rises in vertical currents. Simultaneously, the warm, lighter air is replaced by colder air in descending currents. The airplane is caught in the middle of these two opposing currents. Under these conditions, a very strong, stiff wind coming head-on can literally stop the plane. (This happened to me during my training for the Second License. I will give the details of this adventure later on in the book). To avoid the most violent air currents, in the summer the students didn't fly from 10 am to 4 pm, the hottest part of the day.

Those student pilots who unexpectedly found themselves in the middle of air currents without having been forewarned, could become petrified. While I was attending the funeral of someone in our air field, I met up with Ruggerone, who had made the first flight around the Cathedral of Milano in 1910. He told me that prior to his first encounter with air currents, he had flown only in the winter in the mountains. He encountered air currents for the first time while flying over a relatively large town where the roof tiles produced large air currents. This first taste of air currents scared him so much that he could do nothing but recite every prayer that he could think of, keeping his eyes on the locket of the Madonna around his neck, as if to say, "Help me". He ended up overcoming his fear and surviving the flight. But then, if only those without fear flew, no one would fly. When you got a good handle on them, air currents could be lived with, and talking about our experiences with them was a great pass-time. What took us off guard was encountering them by surprise. Thank God that nowadays students are forewarned of them by their instructors.

TOUR OF THE FIELD

Having mastered the Long Run, we began our fifth exercise, called the Tour of the Field. We would circle around the entire field, both clockwise and counter clockwise, just to get used to going both ways. At the end of the flight, we would be at an altitude of about 600 to 900 feet and we would try to land at our point of departure by throttling down the engine and gliding down in a straight line with the wings level. After we learned how to make a straight glide, we had to learn how to make descending turns. First a quarter turn to the left and to the right, then a half turn – also called a "one-eighty", then a complete turn – called a "three-sixty.

I was still working on my Tours of the Field and trying to master the landing with a straight glide, when I was ordered, by mistake, to make the "Half Hour Flight" which normally came much later in our training. In the Half Hour Flight the pilot climbed to about 3,600 to 4,500 feet and went farther from the field. I'll describe the Half Hour Flight in more detail in another section. Anyway, instead of calling attention to the fact that I wasn't really trained for the Half Hour Flight, I snatched the opportunity to go on it. I guess the outcome was predictable. I found myself unable to bring the plane down because landing with a straight glide from that altitude required experience, and I had not yet mastered descending with turns. I could have glided straight down to about 600 feet, throttled up the engine to bring the plane closer to my landing destination and then glided straight to Malpensa from the lower altitude – but that would have been too humiliating. I remembered having heard that from 3000 feet above the Oleggio Bridge it was possible to make a straight glide all the way to Malpensa. I therefore went to the Oleggio Bridge and started the glide. Unfortunately, I mistook the hangars at Vizzola, which were close, for those at Malpensa and made such a steep glide that my ears were ringing from the speed of the descent. Finally, I landed at Vizzola and from there flew on to Malpensa.

What an emotional experience that flight was. It was the first time that I had climbed to such an altitude. The month was September and it was sundown. I found myself in the middle of an immense cylinder of light, white and golden higher up, and darker lower down until it became violet. Above me was the clearest blue sky. In front of me, far away, the massif Monte Rosa, solemn and joyful, like a huge, friendly giant. Closer to me on the right, resembling an emerald goblet, was Lake Maggiore, and my home town, Intra. It was so beautiful that it brought tears to my eyes and evoked in me a sudden urge to praise God.

After that memorable flight, I got into the habit of reciting my morning prayers on the plane. I enjoyed them more that way. In the future, when flying becomes more routine, it should be possible to celebrate mass on it. After all, where can you find a church more beautiful than the sky?

I feel certain that flying has made me a morally better person, because it has taught me to face dangers voluntarily and serenely day after day, because it has taught me to appreciate the beauty of nature, and because it has given me a sense of the infinite. Being alone in the imposing immensity of space has made me aware of the creator. The sense of the infinite is the greatest pleasure flying provides. But to really enjoy it, you have to fly alone. The presence of someone else destroys the mood. Thoughts such as these made me all the more determined to get my pilot's license.

But let me describe another experience I had while practicing my Tours of the Field. One morning, I climbed to 900 feet to practice my half turns. It was the beginning of October, a beautifully clear morning. Suddenly, while I was in the process of trying to climb higher, a very thick fog formed over the entire air field. It was a marvelous sight. It was like flying over a white sea of cotton made even whiter by the blue sky above. I kept flying without realizing how far I was straying from Malpensa. Suddenly, the fog was behind me and I could see both the Cascina Costa and the Vizzola Air Fields.

Now, how do I get back to Malpensa? No one had warned me that it is almost impossible to land in the fog without slamming into the ground. I had imagined that I would be able to see the ground from a distance of several feet and that I would be able to land as usual. I obviously had not reckoned with the speed of the airplane which devours several yards in an instant. I started my descent with a half turn. At about 300 feet I entered the fog. I could no longer see anything and suddenly feared slamming into the ground without ever seeing it. I straightened the plane and saw the green tops of the trees pass under me at a distance of about three feet from the wheels of the plane. I climbed out of the fog again and enjoyed myself a little while longer flying around that sea of cotton. Then I noticed that mine was the only plane in the air but that another plane had landed just outside the air field's perimeter. It was surrounded by a small crowd of people. I decided to follow suit and tried to land right next to it. Miraculously, I managed to stop just a few feet away from the parked plane barely missing the group of terrified people scattering in all directions.

After landing, I soon discovered that the people were actors dressed up like ancient Romans for the shooting of a film. I then learned that the pilot of the other plane was my instructor and he was not at all pleased by the fact that I had almost killed the actors. He therefore decided to fly my plane back to Malpensa himself because he didn't feel confident in my ability to bring it back safely. So while I waited for him to come back and pick me up, I sat around like a Roman general with my headgear and my tinted goggles taking in the admiration of his tribunes. Now that would have been material for a real film.

When I was later told exactly what had happened, I realized just how lucky I was. Apparently, during my descent I had brushed against the roof of the barracks and was aiming straight for a line of planes parked on the ground sending a number of students scurrying off in different directions. Instinctively, I throttled up, pulled up the nose of the plane, and skimmed the tops of a nearby patch of trees. While all this was going on, everyone assumed I was performing these fancy maneuvers intentionally. The senior pilots jokingly suggested that having landed safe and sound in such a fog, I should have been awarded my license with no additional training. Actually, I owed my life to Saint Elia who had piloted for me. I'll tell you more about Saint Elia later on.

HALF HOUR FLIGHT

With our final exercise, the Half Hour Flight, we started to do some serious flying. We flew around the vicinity of the field for a half hour to forty-five minutes at an altitude of 3,600 to 4,500 feet. We were supposed to stay close to the field so that even if our engine died, we could land at the field with a straight glide. It was calculated that a straight glide was achievable from a distance of about ten times the plane's altitude. So, for example, if we were flying at 3,000 feet, we could go about 30,000 feet or 5.75 miles from the field. But of course, these were theoretical calculations. Reality was another matter. In practice, only the very experienced pilots had a chance of making such a flat glide without ending up skidding on one of the wings. The less experienced pilots were lucky to succeed with the glide only with a distance-to-altitude ratio of six or seven to one. For example, from the Malpensa Field, when we climbed to 4,500 feet, we knew that we could go only as far as the Castelletto Bridge on the Ticino River (a distance of 5 ¾ miles for a distance to altitude ratio of 6.6) in order to have a chance of returning to the field safely with a straight glide.

By this time, provided our engine didn't die, we were all experienced enough to have a good feel for what it took to land safely and with precision inside the field. Part of the learning process was to make the best possible use of prominent landmarks on the ground. For example, I became so good that when I was above such and such landmark at 900 feet, I always started my double turn; and when I was above the widow's house at 450 feet, I always started my half turn. Using the same steps time after time, I could land within 30 feet of my destination, the end of the line of parked planes.

The Half Hour Flights were beautiful because to the north we had a view of the magnificent circle of the Alps and Lake Maggiore. It was a remarkable sight that could only be enjoyed from an airplane. When you're on land, the pre-Alps hide the Alps from view. And when you're in the mountains, the peaks closer to you hide the ones farther away. But from an airplane, in the middle of the sky, you can see everything at once. The Alps rise up above the pre-Alps, and you can appreciate them in their entirety – a crowd of friendly giants whose only function is to keep you company. On windy days, especially, the visibility was exceptional. The distant peak of Monviso looked like it was two steps away and the icy glaciers acquired a vivid splendor (see Figure 4). It must be very dull to fly without the mountains in front of you.

When we were waiting our turn to go on our Half Hour Flight, we stretched out on the ground laughing and joking constantly. Every so often you heard someone scream "airplane". That meant that one of the airplanes coming back from the Half Hour Flight was off course and was heading straight toward us. Some ran off in different directions. Others lay flat on the ground so that they wouldn't be decapitated by the propeller. Either choice had its dangers. Those who ran off sometimes got hit full on the chest by the wing and went flying head over heels.

I learned a lot about sense of speed at higher altitudes from the Half Hour Flight. In the air, when there are no clouds around, you have no sense of speed. You feel the speed when you take off at 60 mph, but as you get farther and farther away from the ground, you have less and less of a reference point for velocity. And when you're at three, six, nine thousand feet up, you feel that you're not moving at all. From these heights, though, you can see hundreds of miles away. You can see your destination one or two hours before arriving and at times you feel like you will never get there.

On the other hand, I certainly had the feeling of speed up high when I flew among the clouds. Whenever I saw a little cloud in the middle of the sky, I would head straight for it! But whereas from a distance the cloud appeared dense, when I got in the middle of it, it would often turn out to be a very thin fog, which was very quickly behind me. There were also the layers of clouds, maybe as deep as 3,000 feet.

Flying through those layers was very depressing. The throbbing of the engine was three times louder than usual due to the humidity and seemed to be warning me of impending danger. I could no longer sense the degree of inclination of the airplane, and I was always afraid of falling. I had an actual experience of this kind with the clouds while training for my Second License. I'll tell you about that a little later on.

I very much enjoyed the feeling of speed when I accompanied the famous test pilot, Pensuti, in determining the speed of the Caproni. We would measure the time required to cover about half a mile, marked by two poles, flying about six feet above the ground. We would fly alongside each other in separate planes and I was in charge of the chronometer. I certainly felt our speed of 80 miles per hour when I saw the ground rush past beneath us. What it must be like today with airplanes that can do 420 mph!

Figure 4 – Flight over the Alps.

FINAL TESTS FOR THE FIRST LICENSE

Actually, the final tests were a lot easier than many of the aerobatics we had performed earlier. They consisted of performing several figure eights while staying at the same altitude, a Half Hour Flight, and a descent with turns. After we were awarded the first License, we could place those blessed Golden Eagles on our sleeves. I had bought the biggest ones I could find in Milano several days earlier. I even had them trimmed with a red border. I must have looked silly with all that gold and red, but no one was rude enough to mention it.

Unfortunately, on the day my tests were scheduled an airplane couldn't be found for me to use. They were all being repaired. The mechanics finally found an old airplane which no one was willing to use anymore. It could turn only to the right and could climb only to 2400 feet. Nevertheless, I was in such a hurry to get my license, I agreed to take it. After taking off, I tried to pull on the stick as hard as I could to make it climb above 2400, but I failed. And I had to descend making only right turns. Such was the glorious and triumphant end of my training for the First License.

But having finally won those Golden Eagles made me do a crazy thing. On that same day, I went grocery shopping at Somma Lombardo. I had been driven there by one of the enlisted men on a military truck. I was so anxious to show my Eagles to my friends in Milano, that I decided to take a chance and go there overnight. The only way I could make the train to Milano was by asking the soldier to drive me to the train station. I knew, of course, that all of this was strictly against regulation. Asking the soldier to drive me was a misuse of a military vehicle and staying outside the garrison overnight without permission was not allowed. Unfortunately, my escapade did not go unnoticed. It so happened that at the train station I ran into the field Commander on horseback. He frowned at me with disapproval because he knew that he hadn't given permission for any of this. But he didn't say anything, and neither did I. I gave him a good salute and boarded the train for Milano.

As it turned out, I was punished with three days of House Arrest and the loss of three days of earned leave. I spent the three days of House Arrest sitting in front of the barracks at Malpensa looking at the passers-by to see if they noticed my Eagles. The field Commander reminded me repeatedly that I was to remain inside the barracks. But I made the elegant defense that, by law, the area within nine feet around a building was actually a part of the building. He finally gave up.

SAINT ELIA INTERVENED

You can't imagine how often Saint Elia actually piloted for the aviator. The story about my experience with fog during one of my Tours of the Field was just one example. There were many others. Quite often, especially in the first Tours of the Field, the student would come close to stalling the plane and falling. You could see Maurice (as we called the Maurice Farman) moving up and down as if to say, "Fly me straight". But the student didn't know how to "Fly Maurice straight". On the ground, the instructor, surrounded by the other students, would bury his face in his hands to avoid witnessing the events. From minute to minute we all expected to hear the cry, "He's falling. Bring the stretcher". Instead, Saint Elia would take the student by the hand and guide him just far enough in the right direction to save his life. Then when the students would tell the instructor that the pilot was out of danger, he would lift his hands from his face in relief and later would prepare a fitting welcome for the pilot. Only when the poor pilot was on the ground did he become aware of how close he had come to losing his life.

And there were other examples of Saint Elia's intervention. One time, two featherbrains, flying around without paying attention to where they were going, smashed into each other. One lost a piece of his plane's tail and the other lost a piece of wing. I was at the mess hall having a vermouth with a few other officers when we saw pieces of their airplanes falling at our feet. No one but Saint Elia could have brought them down safe and sound. And I couldn't believe that the two of them, as soon as they touched the ground, started to argue with each other about whose fault it was.

Another time, when a friend of mine was at an altitude of 1200 feet, he lost the ailerons of both wings. His plane began falling like a rock. Fortunately Saint Elia succeeded in making the plane hit the ground first at the end of one wing and then at the end of the other. With the shock of impact being absorbed by the wings, the pilot managed to escape with only a pulled muscle. When we came running with the stretcher, still panting after having driven at full speed across the full length of the field, we found our friend calmly photographing the remains of the plane. Naturally, it was customary for the student who was fortunate enough to escape injury in such situations to buy drinks all around.

Now poor Saint Elia has been removed as our Patron Saint and the Madonna of Loreto has taken his place. With all due respect to the Madonna, after Saint Elia performed his duty so faithfully for us throughout the years, and saved our lives on so many occasions, he should have remained our Patron Saint.

ENGINEERS CAPRONI AND PENSUTI

Malpensa was filled not only with students training for their First License but with experienced pilots who had already obtained their Second License and perhaps flown for several years. Many of them were trying to qualify to fly the Caproni 300HP. The Caproni 300HP was the famous large three-engine biplane used for bombardment during the war. It was supplied by the Italians to the Allies (see Figure 5). With time, the three 100HP engines were replaced with three 200HP engines and the plane was called the Caproni 600HP (see Figures 6 & 7). By the end of the war, we had developed the Caproni 900HP, a three-engine triplane (see Figures 8, 9, & 10).

The inventor and builder of these giant planes was an engineer by the name of Caproni. Caproni was a very small, simple man, always smiling, and absolutely crazy about aviation, to which he had devoted his whole life. I got to know him well because in between flights I served as military attache to the planes' test pilots. My job included inspecting the cargo to approve it for the anticipated altitude and checking the barograph upon departure and arrival. I also confirmed the velocity of the plane by flying alongside the test pilot with a chronometer. I've already described how we used to measure the speed of a plane in an earlier section.

I frequently accompanied Caproni on a train to Milano. On those times he would tell me of his future plans. After the war, he wanted to build the Caproni 3000HP with six engines, each of 500HP and to establish regular flights between Europe and the U.S. I know that the Caproni 3000HP was, in fact, built and flown satisfactorily. Unfortunately, it was destroyed in one of its first landings.

The test pilot for the Caproni planes was Engineer Pensuti. No one knew that airplane better than he did. Pensuti seemed to have been created by God for the sole purpose of flying. When there wasn't a plane for him to test, he didn't know what to do with himself. He would just find an old Caproni monoplane and fly around with that. Every student knew that only Pensuti could perform certain turns and aerobatics. This was demonstrated to me very vividly when, on the flight I took with him, he executed a scary maneuver every half mile or so. At times, I would see the far end of one wing almost graze the ground and the far end of the other wing way above my head. And while he was playing these little games, Pensuti always wore a big smile on his face.

But I knew that every daring maneuver was carefully planned by him. He risked nothing. Maybe the reason he never wanted to perform "loops", which are easier than many of the other aerobatics which he performed, is because with loops your success depended as much on the strength and endurance of the plane as on your own skill. Pensuti died while testing a Caproni 600HP. The plane caught on fire and he was unable to bring it down quickly enough.

The death of Pensuti was a great loss for Italian aviation. Caproni and Pensuti really complemented each other. Caproni liked to design planes and Pensuti liked to test them. Who knows what they might have accomplished together if they had had more time. He did leave behind a small plane which he designed but did not have time to test, the Triplane Pensuti (see Figures 11 & 12). It was extraordinarily stable and could land at a very low speed and in a very small space. The plane was tested, gave optimal results, and then was never heard of again.

Yes, we had a splendid little Italian air force at that time and we let it go downhill. There was a huge neglect of the air force for the first few years after the war. A few more years of the same and it would have been dead altogether. Luckily, with the help of Marshall Italo Balbo, we were able to restore the air force and elevate it to the height it has now achieved.   Caproni was able to build new planes, one more beautiful than the other.

Figure 5 – Model 1915 Caproni Biplane, 300HP with 3 engines. At that time, it was the largest bomber of the Allied Forces. At the bow, behind the machine guns, sat the machine gunner. Behind him were the two pilots, seated side by side, each with his own controls. The mechanic was standing in between the two engines. The cage with the machine gun in the rear was added in 1916. Note that the cockpit is in front of the wings and unenclosed.

Figure 6 – First edition of the Model 1917 Caproni Biplane, 600HP, with 3 engines.

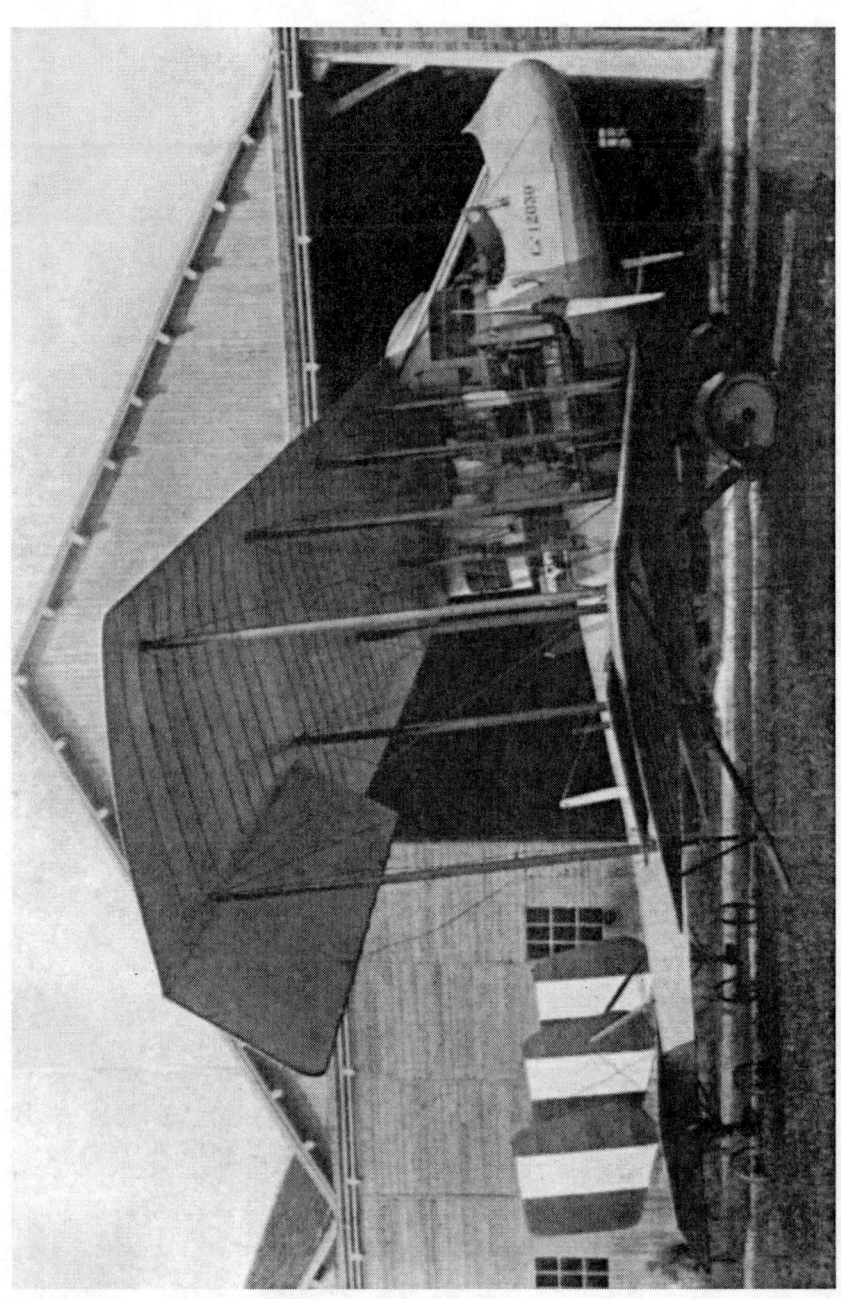

Figure 7 - Second edition of the Caproni Biplane, 600HP, with 3 engines. On this edition the cockpit was modified.

Figure 8 – Model 1917 Caproni Triplane, 900HP, with 3 engines. Used for bombardment. To show its massive size, they placed the Sva in front of it. The Sva was the plane used by D'Annunzio on his Raid over Vienna in 1918.

Figure 9 - Model 1917 Caproni Triplane, 900HP, photographed from the rear.

Figure 10 – Model 1917 Caproni Triplane, 900HP, photographed in flight.

Figure 11 - Model 1918 Pensuti Excursion Triplane. Pensuti never completed testing it.

Figure 12 - Model 1918 Pensuti Excursion Triplane in flight.

OTHER MALPENSA ADVENTURES

As noted earlier, in addition to the students, there were many experienced pilots at Malpensa who already had their Golden Eagles, their bigger paychecks, and their privileges. They roomed at Gallarate where they enjoyed the convenience of frequent trains that would take them to Milano for an evening's entertainment. They had their own special little truck and they came and went pretty much as they pleased.

Despite the huge difference between our standards of living, the senior pilots never put on any airs, looked down at us, or made fun of our blunders. That's because they knew that all it took was a few seconds of distraction, for the experienced pilot to kill himself just as easily as the novice. I remember one day when a senior pilot did make a caustic remark to a student who always seemed to be on the verge of killing himself in practicing the landing for the Short Run. His remark was met with an icy silence of disapproval by the other senior pilots. Harsh criticism, they knew, could easily dishearten the student and contribute to his death. Actually, many of the senior pilots were very kind to us and went out of their way to help us. I remember Captain Salomone, who had earned a gold medal for returning from a bombing mission in which he was wounded and his companions killed by enemy fire. He sat next to me in the mess hall and sort of took me under his wing. From him I learned a number of things that my instructor had failed to mention and I could always count on him to patiently explain what I didn't understand. He was killed later during another bombing mission.

* * *

The instructors were generally enlisted men and somewhat older. Even the officers, such as myself, genuinely respected them. They were very solicitous and at times even paternal. Typically, while one of the students practiced his flying maneuvers, the instructor critiqued his performance and all the other students listened carefully to learn from his mistakes.

* * *

One day a Caproni was flown in from Vizzola to be used by the senior pilots to make practice flights with their instructors. We decided to have a competition among the students to see who could spin the propellers the fastest to start the engine (see Figure 13). You can see that we had to wear our headgear to protect our heads from the sharp edges of the propeller. All of us hung around whenever a Caproni landed in the hopes of hitching an exciting ride.

* * *

One day, an order came stating that every Caproni flying to the squadron, that is, to the front, had to carry a student pilot as a passenger to give him the experience of a long flight. Luckily, I succeeded in being one of the first students to go and had a beautiful three hour flight from Malpensa to Pordenone. Because it was cloudy, we had to fly low for the entire trip. I continuously plotted our course on the map, showing it to the two pilots on board with me. Even though they had flown it several times before, they pretended that I was helping them. When we arrived at Pordenone, I was impressed by the flat, wide landing strip which could be used even in conditions of poor visibility. It was a pilot's dream.

I stayed at Pordenone for some time with another student pilot who had come as a passenger on another Caproni. They kept us there because the men scheduled for an upcoming bombing mission – men who had been schooled in the use of machine guns and bomb launchers – had not yet arrived, and they were planning to substitute us in their place. We looked forward to the prospect of being pitted against the "secular enemy" and hoped to measure up very well. Unfortunately, the bombing mission was canceled and we were sent back to Malpensa by train. The army officers who were traveling with us were amazed to hear that the trip, which required a full day by train, had taken only three hours by plane. They were also amazed to hear that the cargo on the Caproni included not only the two pilots and myself but all their baggage, a dog, and a cage with a pet canary. Incidentally, I've never seen a dog as happy as that one when his feet touched the ground.

* * *

One time, during the summer, General Maggiotto was at Malpensa inspecting the cavalrymen. Upon landing from one of my Short Runs, a classmate helped me bring my plane back to the starting point and I was about to deplane and let some one else fly. Suddenly, I heard pawing on the ground behind me. I turned around and saw General Maggiotto heading toward my plane on horseback. Had he come closer, the horse would have turned into scrambled eggs. I pushed full throttle and took off, flew around the field and landed again. My classmates later told me that the horse was flabbergasted when the plane took off right before his eyes and that General Maggiotto was thoroughly amused by the whole incident.

* * *

Despite the inherent dangers, the fact was that everyone at the field ended up flying as a passenger at one time or another. There was one man, though, who was absolutely determined not to fly. He was a Lieutenant and Doctor for the Malpensa Field. He said that he couldn't fly because he was married and because an elder in his family had warned him not to risk his life for just a little fun. As it turned out, he nearly cost me my life, although not on purpose. I went to see him one day because I wasn't feeling well and he recommended that I drink half a glass of castor oil. Not the refined castor oil sold at the pharmacy, but the gray kind that was used to lubricate the engines. It would make me feel a lot better he said. I drank the oil just before it was my turn to fly. At 900 feet I became so nauseous that I had to come down very quickly and had to quit flying for the day. It wasn't until the following day that I felt like my old self again and realized that I could easily have fainted up there. In those early days of aviation, even castor oil could be lethal.

Figure 13 – Starting the propeller of a 1915 Caproni, 300HP.

THE SECOND LICENSE

BUSTO ARSIZIO AIR FIELD

I was sent to Busto Arsizio to train for my Second License in the middle of November, 1915. What a completely different atmosphere from Malpensa. At Busto, we were treated like kings. There was no one above us, because as soon as a pilot received his Second License, he was either sent to the squadron at the Mirafiori Field near Torino or he returned to Malpensa to train for flying the Caproni. So at Busto, there was just a small group of students plus two instructors and one chief pilot, and we all felt like a part of a close knit family. What we had in common were those precious Golden Eagles of which we were very proud. I remember one time, though, a friend of mine was mistaken for a member of the Voyagers of Colombo because his Eagles looked a lot like pigeons. He felt a little foolish.

We practiced on the Maurice Farman model 1914 plane which was used to both reconnoiter and direct artillery fire. The Model 1914 was similar to the 1912 but without the stabilizer. In the 1914 model, the cockpit was situated forward with the wings completely behind you (see Figure 14). When you flew on the Model 1914, you felt that you were on a balcony in the sky, with full circle visibility and a wonderful sense of the infinite surrounding you. It was as if the plane didn't even exist because it was all behind you. Since we didn't even have a windshield, the air slammed in our face and made our nostrils quiver. We always wore a stocking cap underneath our headgear and kept our mouth shut tight. Only our eyes and noses were exposed to the air. And with that wind in our face, I would guess that we had more fun at our 60 mph than do pilots of today at their 200 mph plus. Alone in the sky, surrounded by the wind, we flew like eagles. Like sea gulls. So flying was beautiful for us in those days as long as everything went well. On the other hand, if the plane nosed down during landing there was the danger that our faces would be smashed against the ground and that the engines, which were behind us, would slam into our back.

Note that other planes in those days also afforded this wonderful visibility (Figures 15, 16, 17 & 18). And note the contrast between our planes and the modern Caproni planes. On the modern Caproni planes the cockpit is situated in front of the wings but it is totally enclosed (see Figure 19) which, it seems to me, would make you feel more like you were taking a trip on a train than on a plane. Moreover, I would think that the wings and the engines are situated forward enough to obstruct the lateral visibility somewhat. Of course the enclosed cockpit does give the pilot much more protection.

The training at Busto did not include any Short Runs or Long Runs. Initially, three or four students plus the instructor would be assigned to a plane with dual controls. We then flew solo on many Tours of the Field and Half Hour Flights at various altitudes and under different atmospheric conditions. Our constant goal was to increase the flying time. Finally came the tests of the *Rectangle*, the *Rate of Ascent*, and the *Raid*. The Rectangle consisted of landing from 3,000 feet within a narrow rectangle. The Rate of Ascent simply meant that you had to climb to the 3,000 feet required for the Rectangle test fast enough to please your instructor. The Raid consisted of making a four hour cross country flight – two hours out and two hours back – with a landing at an unfamiliar air field. The Raid represented the virility toga for the pilots. After the Raid, we were qualified to put the Royal Crown on our Golden Eagles and proceed to the front to do our duty. I'll describe these tests in more detail later on.

Figure 14 – Maurice Farman Biplane, Model 1914. Note the absence of the stabilizer, in contrast to the 1912, and the full visibility in front of the cockpit. Maximum horizontal velocity was 64 mph. Maximum climb was 6000 feet in 22 minutes.

Figure 15 – Voisin Biplane of 1914 which, along with the Farman 1914, was one of our first war planes in 1915. Used for reconnaissance and bombardment. Maximum velocity was 66 mph. Maximum rise was 6,000 feet in 25 minutes. Note that the cockpit is in front of the wings and the full visibility, as in the Farman.

Figure 16 – Bieriot Monoplane of 1915. Maximum velocity of 57 mph. Maximum rise of 6,000 feet in 50 minutes. It stopped being used in war in 1915 because it carried very little cargo and rose very slowly. However, it was a very agile plane, and was therefore used in the first aerobatics. Here also the cockpit is in the front, in fact above the wings, and the visibility is full.

Figure 17 – Savoia-Pomilio Biplane, a 1916 Italian version of the Maurice Farman. The cockpit is similar to the one in the Farman 1914.

Figure 18 – Cockpit of the Savoia-Pomilio 1916, similar to that of the Maurice Farman 1914. Note how it protrudes in front of the wings. This really made you feel that you were on a balcony in the sky.

Figure 19 – Modern Caproni monoplane with two motors. Used for bombardment at night. The cockpit is in front of the wings but is totally enclosed. It's like being in a railroad car in the sky.

ENGINES

In addition to the many other hazards, we flew under the constant threat of engine failure. Engine breakdowns were the order of the day; they happened all the time. Mindful of this, we made sure we were always close to one of the aviation fields in case we had to land quickly.

In 1915, we were just beginning to phase out the De Dion-Bouton with 80HP and 8 cylinders, and the Renault with 70HP and 5 cylinders. In their place we started to use the Fiat with 100HP and 6 cylinders. In the older engines, gasoline was fed to the engine by the force of gravity from an overhead tank so we never had any problem with the engine not getting enough gasoline. On the Fiat, however, the tank was underneath and the gasoline was fed to the engine by an automatic pump activated by the engine itself. As a result, the pump worked fine when the engine was revved up, but it didn't work so well when the engine slowed down. In those situations we were supposed to use a small hand pump to augment the automatic one. Unfortunately, using the hand pump for any length of time badly skinned our fingers. And when the automatic pump failed altogether, as happened frequently, our hand pumping became desperate. Picture what it's like pumping feverishly with your right hand and steering with your left. And all this going on even during the landing. It was not a lot of fun.

And often, there was a leak in the pressure line which passed the gasoline from the tank to the engine, and then the engine would break down altogether. This was even more likely to happen during hand pumping.

Other engine breakdowns were caused by problems with the magnetos. These had previously been purchased from Germany but were then being manufactured for the first time in Italy because of the war. Believe me, the Italian ones at that time left much to be desired.

Let's face it: In aviation, the engine is everything. If the engine fails in an automobile, no big deal. Get out and have it fixed. But in an airplane, get out means get out from 1000 feet above the ocean, above a forest, above the roofs of houses, or above a maze of electrical wires. Clearly, "to get out" is not always so easy in an airplane. The most inept pilot can fly around the world so long as his engine doesn't fail him while the ace dies like an idiot if his engine fails at a time when it is humanly impossible for him to land.

The only real protection against engine failure is to have a backup engine which takes over when the main engine fails. I expect to see the development of an engine that's substantially lighter and much more powerful than the one we have today, maybe utilizing some other kind of power. If it were powerful enough, it could permit a very slow, vertical landing, as helicopters are capable of.

The Spaniard, La Cierva, with his plane, the *Autogiro*, has already partially accomplished a vertical descent with a gasoline engine. The lift on the plane is achieved by a huge horizontal propeller spinning slowly at 90 rotations per minute. The spinning is induced by a blast of air from a vertical propeller and from the speed of the plane. The horizontal propeller currently permits a landing that is within 3 degrees of vertical and La Cierva is hopeful that he can achieve an absolutely vertical landing. It doesn't seem likely, however, that the Autogiro will be able to achieve a vertical take off. A good thing about the Autogiro is that it can't fall into a spin if the engine fails. When it loses velocity, it simply drops and the air currents generated by the drop start the propeller spinning faster which in turn lifts the plane. Sounds a lot better than getting killed when your engine fails.

Since those days, there has been enormous progress in the reliability of the engines. Today there are engines with over 300 hours on them that are still in use. We couldn't even have imagined such a dependable engine. And some recent happenings in aviation are already pointing to the coming of much more powerful engines. On October 21, 1929, the

German seaplane, "Do X" of Dornier, flew for almost an hour over Lake Costanza with 169 people on board and enough fuel to fly for about 720 miles. I believe the "Do X" has 12 engines, each of 500HP. Now picture what will happen in twenty years as the gasoline engines become more and more powerful. I bet they will be carrying 500 or even 1,000 passengers. And then when a new kind of motor is discovered which allows a much lighter fuel than gasoline, they'll be carrying 3,000 people at speeds of 1,200 to 1,800 mph, for a distance of 2 or 3 times around the world. Laugh if you will, but save this book. Read it again twenty, thirty, or forty years from now, and see if you're still laughing. Maybe what you will find forty years from now is that I had too little vision. Remember all of you who are not yet twenty years old, that none of you will reach sixty without having made several intercontinental flights. Craziness? We'll see.

Talking about the exciting things that will happen forty years from now makes me want to cry because I will be in my grave by then. Actually I'll be in purgatory (let's hope) and will have other things to think about. What makes me sad is that by being born in 1893, I risked brain damage by the clanging noise and the stinking odors of the first engines which traveled at a snail's pace. The only compensation was the admiration of my contemporaries for daring to fly. If only I had been born forty years later, I could have been around at a time when silent engines traveling at much faster speeds don't contaminate the air. At a time when flying is practically the only means of transportation and by far the safest. At a time when the automobile and the railroad have practically disappeared. At a time when children at the museum looking at the automobile, the locomotive, and transatlantic ships turn to their grandfather and say "Grandpa, it's hard to believe that you actually traveled in those things!" Stuff worth being re-incarnated for if it were possible. Sometimes I feel that my generation was the victim of both a bad war and a bad peace. I hope God takes that fact into account when I meet him in heaven.

There is one means of transportation which I believe will survive along with flying. It is the ancient one called walking. I never tire of it.

LANDING AND TAKING OFF

Because Busto was an old rifle range converted into a small aviation field, it could accommodate only a very narrow landing strip. Landing was therefore very difficult and we almost always had to throttle up the engine and try a second time. If the carburetor was defective, the engine, now in idle, didn't respond and we could end up either slamming into the barracks or into a nearby field of Robinias [locust trees]. And so the aviation motto, "Reach for the Stars" was appropriately changed to "Reach for the Robinias".

The first few times, we were all so afraid of landing that when a classmate initiated his glide, all eyes were on him to see if he could land successfully. If he miscalculated his glide – that is, if he was "long" – we would all shout out to him, "Throttle up! Throttle up! You're long".

We used that expression in a metaphorical sense as well. For example, when one of the guys was having a hard time keeping his resolve to break up with a girl and we spotted them together, we would remind him "Throttle up. You're long". I remember one guy who was so tired of throttling up unsuccessfully that he asked the rest of us to shred the letters from his girl friend in a million pieces before he could open them. So every time he received a letter we all shouted, "Proceed to Shred". As you might guess, there was real camaraderie among us. We needed it.

Another serious problem we had with the landing was that of controlling the speed of the plane so as to avoid "nosing down" or "pancaking". If the speed was too high, the plane nosed down – that is, it hit the ground nose first and then, as often as not, executed a series of summersaults. The pilot was frequently very badly hurt, especially if the cockpit was in front of the wings (see Figure 20). If the speed was too low, the plane pancaked - that is, it stalled and dropped to the ground from too great a height, and actually slammed into it in an upright position. Obviously, landing was then and still is today the most dangerous part of flying.

* * *

We had a difficult time in taxiing for take off with the Farman Model 1914. Whereas the 1912 model taxied and took off very smoothly, the 1914 model tended to veer left or right so that it could easily end up spinning around itself, or yawing. The problem was intensified by the fact that the controls of the plane behaved exactly opposite during take off than in flight. That is, to make the plane turn right during take off, you had to give left aileron. During flight, to make the plane turn right you had to give right aileron. With these conflicting handling controls it was easy for the pilot, especially at first, to get completely confused, lose his head, and, in fact, contribute to the yawing.

If the yawing occurred when the plane had just begun to pick up speed, the outcome was correctable. The student would just turn around and start all over again. But if it occurred at high speeds, the plane would slide side to side and end up smashing the wing to pieces against the ground. Fortunately, in most cases, no harm befell the pilot who managed to remain safely housed in the cockpit.

One time though, we saw an amazing yaw which could have taken the lives of several mechanics. The student pilot sped down the runway straight as an arrow. Just as he was about to take off, he turned abruptly to the right and the plane started to spin directly toward the hangars. It didn't occur to him to turn off his engine. Only by an act of God did he avoid being smashed against the building's outer wall. Believe it or not, the cockpit, with the pilot still inside, detached from the plane and slid inside an open window that was just at the right height while the rest of the plane crumbled into the wall. The pilot and the cockpit ended up in the middle of a group of bewildered mechanics scared out of their wits. But they all had a nice visit and God only knows how many bottles of wine the pilot had to buy to pay for his mistake. Needless to say, the pilot was completely unharmed because, as we all know, when the patron saint of the hopeless begins to protect, he protects all the way.

Actually, the unbelievable was almost commonplace in those early days of aviation. A photograph made the rounds of the Allied Forces showing a French reconnaissance plane sitting on top of a very large bomber. It had actually landed there. Miraculously, no one was hurt and neither plane was damaged. The same old patron saint of the hopeless.

Anyway, after a few practice runs, most of us finally learned how to taxi for take off on the Model 1914 without yawing. A few students, however, even on the eve of their final Raid, were still unable to taxi for take off without yawing a couple of times.

* * *

Another headache was engine failure during take offs. When this happened, we had no choice but to immediately turn back and do our best to land. The most likely outcome was that the pilot got badly hurt as the plane slid along the ground on its wings before shattering to pieces.

Sometimes the failure of the engine on take off was caused by a flooded carburetor when the pilot throttled up too quickly. Often, however, the carburetor was simply defective. The best thing to do was to turn on the engine ahead of time and let it run full throttle for a long time to get it as hot as possible. To keep the plane from moving forward while we did this, we did two things. First, we put "socks" on the wheels. The socks consisted of wooden blocks driven into the ground which kept the plane stationary. Second, we had our colleagues hold on to the plane and release it when we were ready to take off. The trouble with men holding onto the plane was that they didn't always release it at exactly the same time, causing the plane to yaw in one direction or the other at full speed. Another problem was that, when the colleagues weren't available to hold back the plane, we were so in the habit of throttling up quickly that we continued to do so even when it wasn't necessary. That, in turn, made even a good carburetor really start flooding.

The flooding of the carburetor followed by a malfunctioning of the engine on take off was responsible for the death of Minister Bokanowsky in France in the early thirties. The pilot tried to return to the field but he didn't have sufficient altitude to make the required 180 degree turn. The plane began to spiral, the pilot didn't think of turning off the magneto, the gasoline tank ruptured as it hit the ground, and they all went up in flames. Fortunately, they say that the heat of the flames was so intense that their hearts stopped beating before they burned to death. A less painful death.

* * *

A lot of progress has been made since 1915 in reducing the risk of landing. I've even heard of a 70HP German plane that has an instrument that permits it to fly and land at a speed as low as 6 mph. At 6 mph, you can almost land in a town square.

But we'll do a lot better. Imagine a passenger plane that doesn't even need a pilot. It could be controlled from the ground or by another plane flying a few miles behind it. Then imagine that the plane has a rod that can be lowered right before landing. The rod senses the approaching land and then maneuvers the plane so as to always achieve a gentle landing. Actually, I believe that even the planes which require a pilot will have devices for Instrument Landing. Gone will be the days when you kill yourself because your engine dies and you're still miles away from a landing strip. Gone will be the days of spiraling downwards out of control and gone will be the days of nosing down when your plane touches the ground.

Figure 20 - A complete nose down of a 1915 Caproni 300HP. Fortunately only the cockpit was broken to bits and the pilot remained unharmed.

SPIRALING

All of us students at Busto had a mania for climbing too steeply too quickly. We referred to this as "pulling too much" because we climbed by pulling the lever toward us. This could result in the plane stalling and spiraling downward out of control. The experienced pilots were able to climb fast and steep because they could sense the slight oscillations of the plane which precede stalling. We novices lacked that sense and all it took was a blast of wind from the front to put us into a spiral. Now it's true that spiraling was purposely induced as part of our instruction to teach us how not to lose our heads if it did happen. On the other hand, no one knew a sure way to stop spiraling, so most of us tried to avoid it.

I remember the instructors debating about what we should do in case we did go into a downward spiral. Some thought that we should try to make a wider turn while others thought that we should try to make a narrower turn. We didn't look forward to putting these two opposing theories to the test in a real life situation.

Some of the students who experienced spiraling enjoyed it so much that they actually tried to make it happen again. Needless to add, this was not a good idea. Many ended up hitting the ground and hurting themselves badly.

During one flight, when I was at about 900 feet, I saw a plane spiraling beneath me. Because a good friend of mine had taken off just after me, I assumed it was his plane. It appeared that his engine had stopped functioning on take off and he was trying to make a turn toward the landing strip. But because he was still very low, the turn was very flat and difficult to make. In the middle of the turn, he went into an even faster spiral and smashed into the ground. I looked for my friend to come out of the cockpit, but he didn't show. It seemed likely he'd been killed. I saw the Savoia Cavalrymen and the ambulance rushing toward the plane. Then, thank heaven, the ambulance took off for the hospital at Busto. "He's Alive" I shouted happily to myself.

In time, the other planes all landed. But I just kept flying. I wanted to put off seeing the mangled body of my friend whom I had left brimming with health just a few moments before. I continued to climb very slowly and cautiously to 6,000 feet. Having seen my friend spiral to the ground just a little while ago, I had no desire to have it happen to me. The November sky covered with fog and mist, coupled with the plight of my friend, filled me with a sadness I had never experienced before.

Finally, I decided to face the inevitable and go down. That's when I found out that the accident hadn't happened to my friend after all but to another pilot. Even better, the pilot was only slightly injured and was released from the hospital after just a few days.

Contrary to what one might expect, the outcome of a spiraling fall depended more on how the plane hit the ground than on the height from which it fell. The fact is that the velocity with which the plane hits the ground is the same for a plane falling from 60 feet as for one falling from 9,000 feet. If the cockpit hit the ground first, the pilot was a goner. If the wings hit first, the pilot sometimes escaped completely unharmed, especially if the cockpit was situated in front of the wings. Of course, the advantage of falling from a higher altitude was that it gave the pilot more needed time to regain his composure and stop the fall.

Nowadays, many of the spiraling problems we had in 1915 have been greatly alleviated. I've even heard of an instrument, still not in general use, called the "Artificial Horizon" which helps to maintain the plane's equilibrium and thus prevents spiraling.

THE ELEMENTS

You might well imagine how many problems the clouds, fog, and wind got us into. I will recount just a few.

* * *

Let's start with a cloud story. It was a day in November and the sky was covered with low flying clouds (see Figure 21). I entered the clouds at an altitude of about 1,200 feet at a very long distance from the field. I had made the decision earlier that, for the first time, I would stay in the clouds for at least fifteen minutes.

That was the longest fifteen minutes that I have ever lived through. In the humidity, the rumble of the engine grew louder and more ominous. The clouds were so thick that I could barely see the tip of the wing. To top it all off, it was very cold. Not being able to see land, I couldn't determine the altitude of the plane. All I could do was use my intuition. And if my intuition failed me, I knew I was headed for my eternal rest. But my fear of fear winning over me was stronger than my fear of the eternal rest. At first, I looked at my watch every minute. Then I decided to stop looking at my watch so that I wouldn't lose the "feeling" of the plane. But I ended up looking at it every once in a while anyway. Five minutes passed, then ten, and finally, at fifteen, I took a deep breath and started my descent. I throttled down the engine, the carburetor choked up, and finally the engine stopped altogether. I was in real trouble; I had no choice but to land as soon as possible. Coming out of the clouds at about 900 feet, I discovered that the field was nowhere in sight and nothing looked familiar. I saw nothing but woods underneath me, and I had to quickly decide where to land.

When you find yourself in the middle of the dance floor, you better dance. I spotted a clearing, barely larger than the plane, in the middle of some tall trees. I hovered for a couple of minutes and then brought the plane nose down into the middle of the bamboo canes which filled the clearing. I heard the sounds of the crackling canes and of the mangled plane as it came to rest on them. I was cradled safe and sound by the canes only a couple of inches from the ground.

Under normal circumstances, I could never have executed such a maneuver. It was nothing short of a miracle that I brought the plane within less than a foot from the trees, with little enough speed over the clearing to fall of its weight into the bamboo canes. My only explanation is that during those few seconds my instinct for survival sharpened my senses. In fact, when my instructor flew to the scene to see what had happened to me, he could not believe that I had managed to land that plane in that small clearing from 900 feet up. As for me, I was so proud that I asked him to take several photographs of the plane with me in the cockpit (see Figure 22).

The mechanics came to disassemble the plane which, short of chopping down half the forest, could not be removed in any other way. To ward off the November chill, they decided to gather some logs and build a fire. The farmer who owned the land presented a bill for the wood to the field Commander. The Commander refused to pay it, and the farmer then presented the bill to me. Feeling that my paying the bill made as much sense as serving cauliflower at afternoon tea, I also refused to pay it. As it turns out, the end of the story played out several years later. I was at an elegant dinner party in which every guest was assigned a servant to attend to his needs. I immediately noticed that for some reason my servant had taken a dislike for me and was reluctant to fill my wine glass. The conversation turned to the difficulties of landing a plane in a small area, and I told the story of my landing in a clearing in the Gorla woods. My waiter committed the gravest infraction of his profession when he interrupted me to say, in a loud and proud tone of voice, that the land belonged to his father, who had never been paid for the logs confiscated to make a fire. Once he got that off his chest, the waiter and I exchanged a smile of mutual acceptance and for the rest of the dinner, he refilled my glass even more frequently than was necessary.

* * *

The fog was another one of our big problems. From the beginning of October until spring, the Busto Field was threatened by fog rising from the Ticino River in just minutes without warning. So there was no flying in the winter without dealing with the fog. When the fog extended directly over the field, we didn't fly because we knew there was no way we could return. But when the fog covered only the outskirts of the field, we would take a chance and take off anyway.

The most dangerous kind of fog was one that came late in the day when there were just a few minutes of light remaining and there wasn't enough time to find a better place to land.

Let's move on to one of my fog experiences. It was the first time that I had flown with a Fiat 100HP engine. The plane climbed like an angel to several thousand feet. I was wearing on my wrist a magnificent English altimeter loaned to me by my uncle who was an ardent mountain climber. The instructor had checked out my uncle's altimeter against a very precise one on that same morning and had found it to be right on target. During the flight, I noticed that the regulation altimeter registered a different altitude from that of my uncle but for some reason I paid little attention to the discrepancy.

I was able to see the field so I began my descent with turns going in and out of the clouds constantly. At 900 feet, the fog moved in and I could no longer see the field. I continued down to 300 feet hoping that the fog would be less dense there. I still couldn't see anything and was about to drop to 150 feet. Up to that time I had been using the regulation altimeter. I glanced at my uncle's altimeter and saw that it registered about 60 feet. If it was right, I knew that in just a few seconds I would smash into the ground. I quickly throttled up, straightened the plane, and passed over the top of a clump of trees just a few feet below me. My uncle's altimeter had saved my life. I continued upwards to 150 feet, stayed there until I could see the field through a patch of fog, and down I went.

* * *

As I was landing, I noticed that another plane, an Aviatik, was taking off. It was already fairly late in the evening and I knew that if he wasn't able to land at the field, he was in real trouble because he didn't have time to look for another landing spot. It was clear to me that from the ground, they couldn't appreciate just how thick the fog actually was. And, in fact, almost as soon as the plane took off, it disappeared into the fog. The pilot was a nice sort who came from a town very close to mine. On his time off in between flights, he would go hunting around the field using someone else's gun without permission and my bicycle – also without permission. It was rumored that he mistakenly once took a shot at the wing of a plane as it was landing.

Anyway, my premonitions soon proved to be justified. The pilot was lost in the fog. Within a few minutes we heard the first rumbling of his motor as he circled the field looking for a place to land. But by now the entire field was covered. As I said, it was almost nightfall and the poor guy no longer had the option of trying to find another place to land. We all felt so bad for him as we heard the sound of the plane grow louder as it flew closer and then softer as it flew farther away, over and over again. It sounded like a desperate cry for help and there was nothing we could do to help him. Finally, it was pitch black and the sound of the motor stopped altogether.

We assumed that the pilot had been forced to come down somewhere in the vicinity of the field and we all spread out to look for him. There was little hope of seeing him alive. I was searching along with the field Doctor and another student. It was very cold and the fog was so thick that we kept bumping into the trees. There was mud everywhere so deep that we sank into it up to our ankles. We searched around for about an hour, at times meeting up with other groups who were having no more success than we were. Finally we saw what at first looked like a damaged tree trunk tilted at an angle from having been struck by lightning. On closer inspection it turned out to be the fuselage of the plane (see Figure 23). Then we heard the sound of moans and ran to the scene. Fortunately, the wing of the plane had hit the ground first thus sparing the cockpit and the pilot.

The pilot who was still in the cockpit complained that he felt like everything inside him was broken. The Doctor thought there might indeed be internal injuries so we pulled him out of the cockpit very carefully and laid him on the ground on top of our overcoats. Others went to get an ambulance. I can't begin to tell you what a feat it was to get that ambulance all the way out to the middle of the woods over several inches of mud. By the time we got to the hospital it was very, very late. The doctors examined the pilot very carefully and found that he only suffered a bad case of stiff muscles caused by the pull against his seat belt – plus a scare to last a lifetime. We would have preferred he be sent to hell for all the trouble he had caused but instead he was sent on leave for eight days as happy as a lark. When you think of how many pilots died from a simple nose down of the plane without ever leaving the ground, you realize how very partial Saint Elia was. They tell me that the Madonna of Loreto was even worse. But then, I can't complain about partiality when I think of all the scrapes Saint Elia got me out of.

* * *

Finally, on the subject of fog, I would like to write a few lines about one of our instructors who had an uncanny ability to remain oriented in the fog. He would take off for his test flight first thing in the morning even if he could see the fog beginning to form at the outskirts of the field. On these mornings he would fly right into the fog seemingly without a worry in the world and stayed up in it for about ten minutes. He was content just to fly out in a straight line, make a 180 degree turn, and fly back in a straight line, landing within three feet of his point of departure. Granted he didn't perform any fancy aerobatics, but remaining exactly on a straight line, and making a turn of exactly 180 degrees (a small deviation from 180 degrees would have been enough for him to fly over the field without seeing it) required an ability possessed by few other pilots. Of course, just in case he were to find that the field itself was completely socked in on his return, he always had enough gas to be able to fly for several hours in search of another landing site.

* * *

I also remember many near tragedies brought about by the wind. When the wind was fairly strong, we were told to land into it. If you tried to land in the same direction you ran the risk of being unable to stop and, especially with the small landing strip at Busto, smashing into the wall of the barracks or the surrounding houses.

On one particular day, a very strong wind was blowing. I was ordered to fly first and cautioned to land in a direction opposite to that which I normally took in order to have the wind against me rather than behind me. I will always remember that flight. The wind was in front of me. I was flying with the plane slightly inclined in front, as they say, nose down, to reduce my chances that a sudden strong gust of wind would make my tail drop and send me spiraling. But that wind took hold of my plane and lifted it upward like a kite. I had almost no forward motion. Within 20 minutes, I found myself a very short distance from the field but at an altitude of 10,000 feet, which for those days, was almost unheard of. The sky and the surrounding landscape were crystal clear; the circle of the Alps in front of me had the brightness of steel.

When I decided to descend, I made a 180 degree turn. Immediately after the turn, a gust of wind from the rear suddenly lifted me about 30 feet. I calmed myself quickly, and fearfully continued the glide with much prudence. I finally landed against the wind, in a direction opposite to that which I normally took, and grazed the roof of the barracks in the process. The wind was so strong that I stopped in less than 15 feet with the help of my friends holding on to the plane to prevent it from sliding backward.

Not long after I landed, we were all entertained by the performance of another student. For some reason, he ignored the advice about the wind and attempted to land in the normal direction with the wind behind him. Unfortunately, things didn't go as he hoped. The strong wind just continued to push him forward. Having completely turned off his engine, he no longer had the option of re-starting it and taking off again. We all watched as he approached a string of parked planes unable to stop. The Commander kept shouting, "Yaw, you idiot". Although yawing could probably have saved the pilot from harm and avoided his smashing into the parked planes, he was too far away and the wind was too strong for him to hear anything anyway.

After much yelling and waving, the students flung themselves against the plane to try to stop it. Unfortunately, they were hit in the chest by the wings and thrown upwards with legs flying. The plane ended up wedged in between two others and all three were completely demolished.

All things considered, it could have been worse. The pilot was unharmed and placed under House Arrest for several days. The Commander refused to talk about the incident again.

Figure 21 – Flight in the clouds.

Figure 22 – My airplane sitting in the middle of a clearing barely larger than the plane. Notice the tall tree trunk immediately behind the wings. The rear wing is leaning against the ground because the carriage is gone. I am standing on the shattered bow of the cockpit. A difference of a few inches and I would have been killed.

Figure 23 – Airplane imbedded in the ground. Students are in the process of straightening it.

OTHER BUSTO ARSIZIO ADVENTURES

In spite of the instructors' constant warnings of the dangers of turns that were too sharp, or too flat, glides that were too steep or too flat, etc., we students managed to perform some pretty dangerous aerobatics just for the fun of it.

One of the craziest things I can remember was scaring the cavalrymen half to death as they rode around the field on horseback. Because there was very little good will between the cavalrymen and the pilots, you could often find at least one crazy pilot entertaining himself by flying his plane eight or nine feet above the heads of the horses, causing them to scatter in all directions while their riders held on for dear life. Their officers complained to our officers and our officers made investigations. But with seven or eight planes in the air at the same time, good luck trying to find out who did it.

* * *

One day a blimp came flying around the Busto Field. The blimp wasn't very popular among the pilots. As far as we were concerned, a blimp was to a plane like a hippopotamus to a racehorse. So we showed our disdain for it by flying all around it, over it, and under it. Some pilots even leaned out the window and spat on it. Unfortunately, with all of the beautiful maneuvers, one of the pilots came so close to it that he nearly hit it. At that point, the field Commander flagged all planes to the ground and as soon as we had landed, called us to assembly.

To imagine what we looked like mustered together, you have to remember that at that time the Air Force had no uniform of its own. All of the pilots came from other divisions, so you saw a sailor next to a cavalryman next to a police officer. To make matters worse, the protective outfit worn in flight was each man's choice. So you would see leather jackets of all different colors, sweaters, overcoats, raincoats, etc. No two dressed alike.

At the assembly, the officers lined up on one side and the soldiers lined up on the other. The most senior officer called the men to attention and presented the troops to the Commander who approached us with a heavy limp due to a leg recently injured in a plane crash. It's a shame that the language used can't be fully reproduced, but it went something like this.

"Who is the .... Who almost flew into the blimp?"
One of the soldiers took a step forward and saluted. The Commander gave him a dirty look and continued.
"You low life. Aren't you satisfied with risking your own life? Do you also have to risk the lives of others? Had you hit the blimp and managed to come out of it alive, you could have been court-martialled and ended up in jail for the rest of your life. You should thank God in heaven that I am letting you off with only three days suspension from flying. But beware that the next time you try anything like this, I'm going to throw the book at you".

Then the Commander continued,
"Who is the ass who was paying so little attention that he almost collided with another plane?"
This time one of the officers stepped forward. The Commander could not say anything negative to him in front of the soldiers. Instead, he gave him a nasty look and in a whisper ordered "Report to me later".

* * *

I guess all of us have experienced a crisis from which we seem to be rescued by pure luck. Something like that happened to me. My parents (what will they think when they read this) had bought me 200 Austrian crowns right after the beginning of the war. They wanted me to have the money in case I became a prisoner of war and had to bribe the guards for food. My mother had even made a pretty little pouch to wear around my neck in which I was to keep the money hidden. In front of the pouch she had sewn a medal of the Madonna.

At the end of one particular month in which I was flat broke, I happened to be in Milano with a friend who was in the same situation. All of a sudden I remembered the crowns I had in the pouch around my neck and wondered if the money brokers would still buy them and at what price. I walked into one of the brokerage shops and was offered ninety liras for 100 crowns. I was wearing 180 liras around my neck. I unhesitatingly made the exchange and, as I was leaving the store, shouted happily to my friend, "Long Live Austria". It was 1915, the war was in full swing, and I was afraid that my comment had put me in danger of being attacked by anyone who might have overheard, but we were both officers and in good humor, so no trouble arose. I don't know what the moral of this story is, but if I had been a good, obedient son and held onto those crowns, I would have ended up with nothing because they were later completely devalued.

* * *

As if we didn't have enough ways to get killed in those days, we even risked being shot at by our own guns. One time a pilot who was flying airplanes from Milano to the squadrons on the front lines, arrived with a bullet in his propeller from an Italian rifle model 1891. It was well known that many of the men assigned to guard the streets and the bridges weren't used to seeing planes overhead at all. So when they did see one, they just shot at it reflexively regardless of its nationality. The best way to avoid being shot at was just to avoid flying off the beaten path.

* * *

 While I was still working on my Second License, I got a bad case of the Mange. Yes sir. One of the pilots had it and he spread it to others by loaning them his flying gloves – the hands being the most vulnerable part of the body. I borrowed the gloves of one of the pilots who had been infected, and I contracted the disease as well.

I was miserable. At night I couldn't sleep because I was constantly scratching. In the daytime, I risked killing myself because I was flying half asleep. All my friends stayed away from me and called me "Mangy Mongrel". Finally I was sent to the hospital in Milano. The field Doctor had tried to send me sooner, but I wouldn't hear of it until I had received my Second License.

Twice a day, for eight days, I had to take warm baths to remove my peeling skin. Then they smeared me with a black ointment and wrapped me in white cotton. I looked like I was wearing a convict's uniform. They sent my uniform to be disinfected and my Crown and Eagles, which had been shiny and bright, all turned black.

When they discharged me from the hospital. I went to a restaurant to have a good meal with some friends. When I took my gloves off, my friends looked at my black hands on the white tablecloth and pulled back a little horrified. I was too embarrassed to tell them the truth.

WHAT WE WORE TO FLY

The most important item for flying was the headgear. It consisted of a thin steel helmet covered with cork and a khaki cloth. It had a wing in the front which served as a visor. On the sides were two long bands of cloth which buttoned underneath the chin. This kind of helmet saved my life on many occasions and I still have it with the cork all fragmented from the impact of many nose downs. It was made in Great Britain and the brand name was Roold. I am holding onto it to wear when I am able to buy a small plane and fly again.

Nowadays, pilots wear a protective gear on their heads called a casque which is made out of leather and looks much like a stocking cap. Personally, I doubt it is nearly as effective in protecting the head as our old ones had been. Perhaps the casque is adequate because in modern planes the pilot always sits behind the wings so that when the plane noses down, the wings absorb much of the blow, but I still think my old helmet was better.

* * *

We also wore goggles with a wide leather band that covered the nose. The end result was that between the helmet and the goggles, only our mouth was exposed to the air. In the winter, we also wore a stocking cap underneath the helmet to protect the chin and neck from the cold.

Finding the right goggles was very important. I tried various kinds and settled on one made of a single flat piece of glass covering both eyes. This model protected my eyes completely from the wind and offered maximum visibility. The fact that the glass was made of a single flat piece made it easy and inexpensive for the glass blower to replace it when broken. The goggles also had two small pieces of glass on the side for lateral vision.

Some goggles were made of plastic instead of glass. Whereas those broke just as easily as the glass they had the advantage of not shattering into a million pieces and threatening you with blindness – the fourth most common injury in the event of a nose down. The three more likely injuries were breaking your head open, burning alive in gasoline flames, and being crushed by the engine.

The pilots who couldn't tolerate bright sunlight would wear goggles made of colored or smoked glass. These glasses were better for flying above the clouds or when there was snow on the ground because they protected you from the glare. But if you were wearing them during a landing when it was a little dark or a little foggy, they posed a real problem because you couldn't see the ground.

If it was raining or snowing during a landing, we always had to remove our goggles because the accumulation of the water and ice on the lenses reduced visibility to almost zero. Remember that we flew without a windshield, and without a windshield at those speeds, the rain drops and snow flakes felt like stones bombarding our eyes and the small part of our face that was exposed.

In the air, however, we could continue wearing our goggles provided it wasn't raining too hard. The visibility was reduced but it was still better to wear them than to endure the pounding rain in our eyes. Time permitting, we could escape the snow by rising above the clouds that produced it but then we were faced with the extreme cold at the higher elevation. If we had no choice but to remain in the snow, we had to remove our goggles to prevent the accumulation on them that made it impossible to see anything. Then we would fly around with our eyes half shut praying to God to help us endure the pain. As back up, some pilots brought goggles with steel lenses with them. Each lens had three small slits in it that permitted a little visibility and at the same time protected the eyes from the snow. After a while, though, even the steel lenses got clogged up. In short, there was just no good solution to the snow problem other than St. Elia helping us utilize our best instincts (actually, most tragedies resulted from foolish blunders during routine flight operations when no particular danger seemed imminent).

There were some pilots whose cornea was so hard that they were able to fly in fairly severe conditions for hours without wearing goggles. On the other hand there were others whose eyes were so sensitive that they bled after flying for just a few minutes. The only man I know who didn't need goggles at all was my cousin and classmate, Edoardo Scavini (see later section containing a letter written by Edoardo describing a bombing mission). He flew throughout the entire war without wearing goggles flying for as long as five hours at a stretch. He was very well known for having earned three silver medals. His brother, a pilot as well, also earned three silver medals. The two brothers set a record in aviation for the most silver medals earned by two brothers. Edoardo also participated in the first flight from Rome to Tokyo in 1919. It was the longest flight ever made up to that time.

Nowadays, of course, flying in the rain and snow is much more comfortable. The cockpit is covered and is equipped with a windshield wiper like they have in cars.

* * *

The clothing we wore depended very much on the season. In the summer, when it was hot, we flew wearing a shirt made of a combination material, often without a jacket. It felt wonderful to leave the hot moor below and climb to the coolness of 6,000 feet. In the winter, on the other hand, we faced temperatures of near freezing on the ground and 5 to 15 degrees below zero at 12,000 feet, so we wore a very heavy sweater, a leather jacket, an overcoat or a cape, and a hat.

Whether you had an overcoat or a cape was very important that winter. The overcoat was preferable and the heavier and longer it was the better. When it was very cold, those who didn't have an overcoat tried to borrow one from someone else. I had the heaviest and longest one imaginable. My overcoat was particularly desirable for pilots who were about to go on their final Raid because they had to stay up in the air almost the entire day. Moreover, if there was fog over the air field when they tried to land, they might have to land somewhere else and stay out several additional days. So that winter I often swapped my overcoat for many more elegant ones and for many different kinds of fancy capes. By the end of the winter my overcoat was worn and faded from having been scoured several times to remove the stains of the motor oil. I really became angry at one of my friends who borrowed my overcoat to go on his Raid and returned it with a big tear in the sleeve. He said it got there from rubbing against the edge of the cockpit for three hours while he used the manual pressure pump because the automatic one wasn't working. He did have it rewoven by a group of women who were famous for being able to patch anything. You could still more or less see where the tear had been though and it made my overcoat much less elegant than it had been. And that is the story of how I sort of alternated from rags to riches in my attire that winter.

Our need for heavy clothing was due to the fact that the plane left our bodies completely exposed from the waist up. And even from the waist down, our only protection was the insulation provided by the cloth which lined the floor and sides of the cockpit. But the cloth was so thin that the wind came right through it. On the older planes, things were even worse. The Farman Model 1910 had no cloth lining on the sides or the floor. The pilot sat on a little stool in front of the motor over the lower wing (see Figures 24 & 25). The Farman Model 1912 had no cloth lining on the floor whatsoever. There was just a rack of steel through which we could see land below. Some pilots became very dizzy if they looked down through the floor. The pilots who flew the Aviatik were generally kept warm by the motor which was in front. Those who flew the Salmson were kept even warmer because the motor in front radiated sparks. If only we could have flown the Farman in the summer and the Aviatik in the winter.

None of the seats on the planes, by the way, came close to being comfortable. Generally it was made out of wood with a short back. After a long flight, our backs and necks hurt from opposing the force of the wind. Had the back been just a little higher, we could have been much more comfortable.

* * *

Another important piece of clothing was our gloves. We had all kinds. Our favorites were the cotton gloves lined with rabbit fur. But no matter how good the gloves, we were never able to fully protect the tips of our fingers from the cold. In fact, among those who were ready to execute their final Raid, there was always some one who suffered permanent injury of his little finger from frostbite.

* * *

One way to keep our feet warm was to put on big wooden shoes full of sawdust over our normal shoes. The trouble with the wooden shoes was that we then had to spend a good deal of time trying to strap the shoe securely to the pedal, which was much narrower. And even when we thought we had succeeded, it wasn't unusual for our foot to slip off the pedal during flight.

Another way to keep our feet warm was to wear several alternate layers of wool socks and socks made of waterproof Japanese paper. Then we put a pair of galoshes over the thick mound of socks without even wearing any shoes. You can imagine how silly we looked in them.

* * *

Another part of the body that could become very painful from the cold was the cartilage in our knees. To protect our knees, we covered them with newspaper. There was almost nothing that protected from the wind better than paper. In fact, paper was so effective that we could buy gloves, socks, chest protectors, and underwear all made from Japanese paper.

We all suffered from cold noses but there was nothing that could be done about that. And of course, those of us with a moustache soon discovered that it was always covered with ice. Our mouths were generally so iced up after we landed that the answer to "how was your flight?" consisted of several unrecognizable stutters from lips too frozen to move.

 One sensation from the cold was very curious. On landing, having gone from, say, 5 degrees below zero to about 40 degrees in a very short time, we felt uncomfortably warm. Indeed, our feet felt like they were scalding when they touched the ground. I remember one guy who on deplaning actually tippy toed around as if he were walking barefoot on a hot pavement.

Figure 24 – Henri Farman 1910 Biplane. Uncle of the Maurice Farman 1912. Note the absence of a cockpit.

Figure 25 - Henri Farman 1910 Biplane. Note the entanglement of tension wires which could easily break if the pilot became trapped in them during his ascent or descent.

FINAL TESTS FOR THE SECOND LICENSE

Finally it was time to ready ourselves for the final tests required to obtain the Second License. As a first step, the instructor listed the number of flying days each student required before he could safely take the final tests.

Some of the men, especially those whose fiancees were at the air field with them, didn't really want to take their final tests because afterwards they would have to go to the front. Therefore, they purposely made flying errors so that the instructor would have to endlessly increase the number of days before the tests could be taken. Such men were called *filibusters* or, in their later stages, *shirkers*.

The term *filibuster* was also used to describe men who didn't want to fly at all but wanted to continue receiving the generous flight pay. Most of these men were married. I remember one old man who had recently been frightened out of his wits during an accident in which he almost broke his neck. After that, he really didn't want to fly at all and would show up for flying exercises only occasionally. And when he did show up, he carried his headgear under his arm, strolled around the planes pretending that he was about to board one, and then suddenly disappeared back into the barracks. He finally managed to get some kind of ground crew job that allowed him to be permanently stationed at the air field.

Surprisingly, the *filibusters* were few. Most of us would have given anything to fly. In fact, the enlisted men often complained that the officers used their higher rank to get ahead in line for taking turns flying.

The tests for the Second License, as I've already mentioned, consisted of the Rectangle, the Rate of Ascent, and the Raid.

* * *

The Rectangle and the Rate of Ascent were performed during the same flight so they need to be described together. For the Rectangle, they etched a rectangle, about the size of a tennis court, right in the middle of the field with lime. The test required that we climb to 3,000 feet as quickly as possible, and glide down without using the throttle to land within the rectangle four times in a row. The time required to reach the 3,000 feet was the Rate of Ascent test and was recorded by a device called a barograph which we carried on board.

The barograph consisted of a small box worn around the neck which contained a time keeping drum wrapped in paper. As the paper unwound, a small pen traced a graph depicting the altitude relative to time. The barograph boxes were generally kept locked so that the pilots wouldn't be tempted to insert their own forged graph. You can't imagine the pride that little box around our necks stirred in us. Wearing it told the world that we were really serious pilots. As soon as we took off, we made sure that the little box was recording. And if it wasn't, we immediately descended to have it adjusted. The results were considered so important that we had to sign the graph to confirm that it was accurate and that we hadn't tampered with it. Another complication: at an altitude above 6,000 feet the pen in the barograph slipped out of its socket and nothing else could be recorded. If this happened during your Raid, the rule was that the rest of your flight didn't count and you had to start all over again.

The infamous French pilot, Callizo, managed to beat previous height records so many times thanks to his fraudulent graphs. Eventually the Commissioner began to suspect him, so he secretly placed a second barograph on one of the wings during one of his flights. It turned out that whereas the height reported by Callizo was 36,000 feet, the height shown on the barograph in the wing was only 15,000 feet. It really ended up badly for Callizo because he had feigned a fainting spell at the "36,000" feet to demonstrate that at that height, even with the oxygen tank he had carried aboard, the fainting couldn't be prevented. He was eventually stripped of all his titles and, if memory serves, even brought to trial.

In trying to climb to the 3,000 feet as fast as possible, we often had to balance our desire to achieve the best time with our desire to stay alive. In trying to reach the height as fast as possible, the inexperienced pilot was prone to "pull too much" and thereby risk the fatal downward spiraling discussed earlier. Even the instructors were torn between wanting us to look as good as possible on the graph paper and being responsible for our safety.

Our performances on the Rectangle tests frequently fell short of perfection. We would touch ground short of the Rectangle, or we would cross the boundaries of the Rectangle on the taxi, etc. etc.. But these so called minor mistakes tended to be overlooked because pilots were urgently needed at the front and because other students were waiting to train on the limited number of planes available. The outrageous result of all this rushing was that the training to be a pilot was almost more risky than the fighting at the front. The percentage of fatalities was enormous. In their Lombardian dialect, the local bourgeois pitifully referred to us as "neck meat", the term applied to animals in the slaughter house.

But we didn't care what they called us. Dying was always for others anyway. Never for us. And we were so full of that inner pride, that unwavering acceptance of danger, that fierce shame of displaying any sign of cowardice. Now that I'm older, I can see that these emotions are present in all young men even when there is no war. It's almost as if for many young men the fear of being afraid is the biggest fear of all. And the most courageous young men, therefore, tend to be those with the biggest fear of being afraid.

You could easily tell the extent of the fear from the way the pilot sat in his cockpit. Hunched forward and contracted, he appeared very much afraid. Reclined backward, as if in an easy chair, he appeared fearless. Thus, we would do our best to recline casually hoping that the position itself would help steady our nerves. Perhaps many other aspects of life involve this same tension between inner struggle and outward appearance.

Obviously, our ascent rates were smaller then than they are today. If the newspapers aren't exaggerating, English fighter planes today can climb to 18,000 feet in 8 minutes. And our modern Italian ones aren't so bad either. By contrast, our Maurice Farman Model 1914 used to take 22 minutes, plus or minus, to climb to 6,000 feet. And the 1912 Maurice Farman had difficulty climbing to 6,000 feet, no matter how much time you gave it, when it was new and to 4,500 feet when it was old. One time, I was flying through a wind that was so strong that it lifted me up like a kite to about 10,000 feet in just 25 minutes. I wouldn't be surprised if I unintentionally broke the ascent rate record with that flight.

* * *

The Raid, as I've already mentioned, consisted of making a four hour cross country flight - two hours out and two hours back – with a landing at another air field. We pronounced it "Raeed", Italian style. It was an exotic, foreign word to us, and it seemed to occupy an inordinate amount of our conversation. "In three days.....", "The day after tomorrow.....", "Tomorrow, I will make my final Raid". But then we'd make some stupid mistake and the instructor would postpone the Raid for several more days.

The only bases within two hours flying time at the speed of about 60 mph were Malpensa, the Taliedo Field near Milano, Cameri, Piacenza, and Torino. (Test flights made on the planes recorded speeds greater than 60 mph but were unrealistic because they were measured with a stopwatch at the beginning and at the end of about a half a mile when the planes were brand new. It was a whole different story when the planes got older and were flown over long distances under changing atmospheric conditions).   Malpensa, Taliedo and Cameri were too close. That left Piacenza and Torino. To go to Piacenza, you simply followed the Ticino River until it joined the Po, and then followed the Po eastward all the way to Piacenza. To go to Torino, you either headed straight for the little mountain peak of Supergo which was visible from the field, or followed the Ticino to the Po and then followed the Po westward to Torino.[see Figure 1]

We were given maps to help us find our way as well as a complicated tool to help us read them. The map consisted of a collection of individual touring guides for the areas which were included in our route taped together to form a long, continuous rectangular piece of paper. The paper was wrapped around a spool which the pilot unwound as the flight progressed.

I found that reading a map from the air was fairly easy. Railroad tracks looked like bright black continuous lines, roads looked like shiny white lines, rivers and canals looked like blue ribbons, and the ground looked like little patches of various shades of yellow and green. As I mentioned in an earlier section, I was also lucky enough to have had a little practice reading a map when I made a three hour flight as a passenger with a couple of experienced pilots on board a Caproni that was going from Malpensa to Pordenone.

Map or no, it was very common for some of the pilots to get lost. This was especially true of the enlisted men who had never read a map before. With all the hurry to enlist pilots, no effort was made to spend time teaching them such things. Nor was it always easy to recognize the railroad tracks, rivers, and main roads beneath us.

In addition to a map, they also gave us large compasses. The compasses, I can assure you, absolutely no one could read. I can remember the enlisted men carrying their compass on board with great pretentiousness although, for all the good it did them, they might as well have been bringing aboard a rock.

Of course, when there was fog, the map did us no good, whether we could read it or not. What we did rely on was our familiarity with all of the mountain ranges of the Alps which were clearly visible when we climbed above the fog. Plus our basic sense of direction which must be similar to that of many flying birds such as pigeons, swallows, and wild ducks. For some reason, it seemed that the less skill the pilot had in reading maps, the better his sense of direction. I guess it's not surprising.

On the Raid, we always had to carry a 155 lb. bag of sand with us in the passenger seat. The sand was there to accustom us to handle the plane safely in case we had an actual passenger aboard.

MY FRIENDS' RAIDS

One of the most memorable people that I met during that year of 1915 was a Genoese who originally came from Montgolfier in France. He couldn't speak Italian. Only French and Genoese which he intermingled to create speech that was barely understandable but very entertaining to listen to. He was the biggest scatter brain that I had ever seen. And he could do nothing without hamming it up. Riding around on the truck he would make motions with his hands and legs as if he were flying on a plane. To this day, I don't know if he actually thought that he was on a plane or if he was pulling our leg. In any case, when we sort of woke him up with a big shove to bring him back to reality, he would laugh his eyes out. He shaved only when the field Commander threatened to order him to go to the barber. He wore a heavy turtle neck sweater that reached all the way up to his ears and covered it with a long, scraggly beard. His hat was always dented because he was either sitting on it or he accidentally left it underneath the wheel of a plane. He looked like anything but an officer.

One day my Genoese friend and three others took off for Piacenza for their final Raid. The trip should have been very simple. Follow the Ticino south to the Po and then follow the Po eastward to Piacenza. The four planes took off all at the same time, each with its pilot and the 155 lb. sack of sand in the passenger seat. They all climbed to 2,400 feet. High enough to fulfill the altitude requirement for leaving the field and at the same time not so high that the pilot couldn't return for a landing if his engine failed. All of a sudden, one of the pilots throttled back and came in for a landing. Everyone ran toward the plane to see what had happened. It turned out that the Genoese had forgotten to place the marking pen on the paper of his barograph. This was serious because if the barograph didn't record, the flight didn't count.

Anyway, he got the barograph pen and departed again accompanied by the laughter of his classmates and shouts from the instructor that he was a mindless scatterbrain. The instructor's final words were "if that one returns tonight, it will be a miracle!" But no one could have predicted where it would all end.

The trip out went smoothly. He followed the Ticino; found the Po; followed the Po; Found Piacenza and the field; landed and dined at the field. When they telephoned us to tell us that all four had arrived, we heaved a sigh of relief.

But on the return trip, things degenerated. My friend followed the Po all right but for some reason, didn't turn north on the Ticino. It was hard to believe that he could miss the turn because it was a clear day and the Ticino is a fairly wide river. It turned out that he mistook the continuation of the Po for the Ticino and just continued to follow the Po on the assumption that he was on his way back home. He finally looked at his map and realized his mistake. By then it was getting dark and he decided to land on a farm near a little town in between two furrows. That he landed without nosing down is in itself nothing short of a miracle.

As soon as he landed, a group of nearby farmers gathered around and he asked them the name of the town. When they told him "Livorno", his response was "This can't be Livorno. Livorno is on the sea". Raving mad, he restarted his engine, taxied between the two furrows, risking nosing down a second time, and took off leaving behind a group of perplexed farmers. It soon became even darker and my friend had to risk nosing down a third time by landing near another town. As soon as he was on the ground, a group of people including the town Mayor and the Chief of Police ran toward the plane. In telling them about his misadventures, my friend learned that in addition to Livorno on the sea there was a Livorno in the Vercelli province. He also discovered that he had landed on the estate of a high aviation official. Everyone considered my friend of such importance that the Mayor invited him to his house for dinner along with the town Priest, the pharmacist, and the school teacher.

Normally my friend didn't drink at all. But as part of the dinner, he told us, they practically forced him to indulge. Towards the end of the evening, the Mayor asked him to give a speech and he, of course, couldn't refuse. What the speech was about he couldn't remember. All he could remember was that they applauded enthusiastically. Drunk and able to speak only French and Genoese. I can't help but wonder about the applause.

Anyway, the next morning he went to his plane to take off and found that his fame had spread. The town school teacher and her students were gathered around the plane. One of the children stepped forward and recited a little tribute entitled "To the Gentleman from Montgolfier". He had to stand up in the cockpit and make yet another little speech. This time at least he was sober.

His story ended happily. He returned to Busto safe and sound but we were in no mood to listen to his story for we were worried about one of the other four pilots who had not yet returned and about whom we had heard nothing since he left Piacenza. Finally, he also telephoned and announced, "I am safe and sound. The plane is in the trees. Come and get it down." He too had gotten lost, nightfall caught him by surprise, he came down in a wooded area, and was lucky enough to bring the plane down safely suspended on a clump of tall trees. And there he remained the entire night cooped up like a chicken inside the cockpit – uncomfortable and hungry – without daring to move for fear that the plane might fall to the ground. He shouted for help as loudly as he could but nobody heard him. Finally, in the morning, some woodsmen happened by and saw him. They tied uprights and struts to the branches and he was able to come down. I have no idea how the mechanics managed to disassemble and remove the plane from the trees.

GETTING LOST

At this point, I can't help but ask myself if the reader thinks that my account of pilots getting lost is exaggerated. Believe me, it happened all the time. Luckily, I have in front of me a book entitled "The Secret of Orientation in Flight" by Antonio Locatelli. In it, he describes an episode which seems even more far fetched than mistaking the Po River for the Ticino. And this didn't happen to a student pilot but to a full fledged pilot at the front. Let me quote directly from the book.

" A very experienced pilot in the war took off on a reconnaissance mission with an observer who had flown little. They headed north, straight for a particular peak in the Alps. At a certain point, the pilot, disoriented by antiaircraft fire, accidentally made a complete 360 degree turn – that is, he really ended up going in the same direction. The observer, who was trying to follow the route with his map, became completely confused by the jumble of snowy peaks which suddenly revolved around him during the turn. And after the turn ended, he was no longer able to coordinate his surroundings with anything on the map upon which he so heavily relied. As a result of the conflict, he was brought to a state of confused panic. The pilot found himself in the same state of mind and the two of them, bewildered, stared at one another. There was a compass on board, but since the pilot had never investigated the meaning of either the letters or the numbers on the dial, it only served to aggravate his confusion. It occurred to neither one to use the shining sun as the reference point to find south and the direction of Italy. Fortunately, they spotted a series of small lakes which they recognized as being in Austria and they made a 180 degree turn. But their confusion was so powerful that they viewed the Italian flat land below as that of the enemy and our aviation fields and planes also as those of the enemy. They didn't even recognize towns and land marks with which they were familiar and over which they had flown many times previously. They finally ran out of gas and the pilot landed in a town which he didn't recognize but which he had flown over regularly for over a year. They managed to survive but they were in a semi-frozen state from the length of time they had spent at such high altitudes. Each man accused the other of being crazy."

MY RAID

By the end of December, 1915, it was finally my turn to execute a Raid. As I've already mentioned, the two possible destinations for our Raids were Piacenza and Torino. Unfortunately, both destinations were normally buried in fog that time of year. And even when there was no fog in the morning, we were afraid that some might form while I was en route. My Raid was therefore postponed week after week. Mid-January of 1916 arrived and I still had not performed my Raid.

 I wasn't the only one who was anxious to complete his Raid. And we all griped that we wanted to get the test over with, put that precious Crown on top of our Golden Eagles and go to the front to do our duty. But despite our impatience, the instructors had to be careful not to send us out on a suicide mission. Day after day, we walked around the stationary planes in the hangars like dogs foaming at the mouth to go on the hunt. Finally, the instructors could no longer take the pressure and a compromise was reached. They agreed to let us fly to Cameri by way of Mortara and Vercelli and land at the field there. This would amount to roughly a two hour trip. On the return from Cameri, we were supposed to fly around the vicinity of the Busto Field for approximately another two hours, thus fulfilling the essential requirements [see Figure 1].

No sooner said than done. Two of us were scheduled to go. In the morning they called the police at Mortara and Vercelli to tell them to be on the lookout for two planes in about an hour and to call the field Commander as soon as they spotted them. First, of course, they double checked with Torino to see if there was fog there and the answer was "yes, very thick". The one who answered the phone at Torino to report on the status of the fog was one of my former classmates who had discontinued the training on the Farman plane to go to Torino to train on the Caudron. (The Caudron was a small plane that gave you great pleasure just to look at it. It was elegant, light, flexible, and could climb faster than any other plane. Now the poor little thing is in a museum, but at that time its ability to climb to 15,000 feet in just a little over an hour was considered fantastic. Our Farman could climb like that only when a frontal wind dragged it upwards like a flying deer. Under normal circumstances, you thanked God if you reached 12,000 feet in any amount of time.)

A short digression: my friend in Torino was famous for always being short of cash. It was a monthly occurrence. On the 27th of each month, he would receive his good sized salary and his flight pay for the whole month. Nevertheless, within a few days he had spent all of his money without having paid his room and board, his barber, or his confectioner. His debts continued to mount but it didn't seem to concern him no doubt because his family was probably paying them off. After he ran out of his own money, he would start to put the touch on all of his friends one after the other. And he was so likeable and had such a gift of gab that he succeeded in borrowing whatever he needed while leaving the giver with a smile on his face. When one of the pilots from Busto landed at Torino on his Raid, the first person under his plane was always my friend. He accompanied the pilot for breakfast and graciously allowed the pilot to pay for both of them. And if later they phoned from Busto to tell the pilot that there was fog there and not to depart, he kept the pilot company all the while that he was in Torino, entertaining him like no one else and, of course, making him pay for everything. Strangely enough, he probably got away with all the mooching because there was such a strong fraternity among the pilots in general. A sort of "what's mine is yours and what's your is mine" attitude about money and everything else.

On we go now with the story of my Raid to Cameri via Mortara and Vercelli. Whereas normally there was an abundance of planes, on that particular day, they were all broken except one. Because there were two of us going on our Raid, they sent me with the instructor to Malpensa to fetch another plane. The instructor did the piloting and I went along as the passenger. The last time that I had been in a similar situation was when I began the course for the Second License and I had to learn to fly the Farman 1914. At that time I had to make three or four flights with an instructor on a plane with dual controls. But even then, I was doing the piloting. The instructor merely corrected my mistakes. Here the instructor was in complete control. I wasn't used to being a passenger and I got scared. Really scared. Although he may have been ten times better than I was, not being in control made me very uneasy. I kept thinking that for all I knew a small gust of wind could have made him lose control. I understand that many pilots have the same problem and that it even happens to people who drive automobiles. Needless to say, I was very happy to land at Malpensa, and equally happy to take off from Malpensa alone in my nice new airplane. The funny thing though was that the fear that sort of gripped me when I was a passenger stubbornly remained with me on the way back when I was alone. Because it had seemed to me that the instructor was "pulling too much" during the flight to Malpensa, I felt fearful that I too was "pulling too much" on the way back. The end result was that whereas the instructor took off after me from Malpensa to return to Busto, he was quickly far above me. What an embarrassment for me who prided myself in "pulling like a demon".

After I landed in Busto, they put the spool with the map of my route in front of me, the barograph around my neck, and tied the passenger sack of sand beside me. The other pilot who was making his Raid with me took off first. Then came my turn. I was so mad at myself for having climbed so slowly on the last flight that I "pulled" like crazy. I overtook the other pilot in a minute and while he was still flying around the field trying to gain enough altitude, I headed straight for Mortara. What a dull route. Instead of enjoying the beautiful Alps, I saw nothing but flat lands covered with trees and furrows. Every once in a while I turned around to see if the other pilot was behind me. I passed over Mortara and turned toward Vercelli. At least now I had at my right the spire of the dome of San Gaudenzio of Novara which rose out of the clouds and kept me company. The dome of San Francesco of Vercelli was approaching quickly and broke the monotony a bit. When I arrived at Vercelli, I flew around the area a bit to make sure the police saw my plane so they could call the field Commander, then headed straight for Novara and Cameri. By this time the other pilot was behind me.

It was as if the dome of San Gaudenzio of Novara was put there just to guide me because I could see absolutely nothing else of the town. Thick fog was everywhere. And now how do I find Cameri? It was shown on the map but at first I couldn't locate it on the ground. Fortunately, the students at the Cameri Field had enough sense to line up all the planes in formation so that I could see them from the air and thus determine the location of the field. Down I went.

I had made the entire flight at 6,000 feet which was the maximum height that could be recorded by the barograph. (Had the barograph stopped recording, the flying time wouldn't count). I started my glide downward. Then, in the middle of my glide, the automatic feeding pump for the engine stopped working. This was the last thing I needed. I don't think I've mentioned yet that my plane was one of the first manufactured in Italy and that it was not unusual for those first planes to experience failure of the feeding pump, or the magneto, or the carburetor, or the engine itself. Adding to my apprehension was the fact that the Cameri Field was completely unfamiliar to me. I prayed that I would land within the field itself rather than in the brush outside. As it turned out I did pretty well. Luckily my initial decisions were on the mark because once my engine died the only thing I could do was to put myself in the hands of the Madonna. My plane came to a stop within three feet of the row of lined up planes.

Everyone ran toward me. I got out of the plane with the air of importance befitting a man who was in the process of making his Raid. The students all took me to breakfast at the field restaurant while the mechanics repaired the feeding pump and refueled my plane. They didn't let me pay for anything because I was a guest of the field. I had a great appetite. I guess the two hours and 6,000 feet had combined to make me very hungry. I took a little nap and chatted with the students who were keeping me company. I finally went back to my plane for my return to Busto. I gave the mechanics two gold liras for their work on the plane. I still feel a little guilty because I think I borrowed the liras from my friend who landed after I did and I never paid him back. My friend had to stay overnight because his engine had died completely and the mechanics couldn't repair it in time for him to return the same day.

As soon as I took off for Busto, I could see that the fog was increasing so I headed directly for the field. Remember that I was supposed to fly for two hours around the Busto Field to fulfill my Raid requirements. From above the field, I could see smoke rising from a fire they had built using the dry brush from the moor. I didn't know if they were doing this to help me locate the field or because they wanted me to come down right away on account of the fog. I flew around the field for a while and decided that since the fire was still burning, they really wanted me to come down without delay. I started my glide, and half way down the automatic pump stopped working again. I didn't have time to start using the back up hand pump. Oh, what a pain. Another landing without an engine. I tried to land in the middle of the field but instead I found myself flying just a few feet above the parapets at the approach to the field. The workers who were trying to carry them away had to duck their heads to avoid being hit by my plane. I couldn't help but wonder why they didn't carry them away sooner. If I had been just a few feet "shorter" I would have slammed against them and have gone to my Eternal Rest. And that would have been the end of these memoirs.

The success of my Raid notwithstanding, I had yet to complete the two flying hours required on my return. Nevertheless, that night I paid for drinks all around because I considered myself as having earned my Second License and entitled to wear the Crown on my Golden Eagles. How embarrassed I would have been if I had put myself out of commission before actually completing the two hours. As it turned out, I put myself out of commission immediately after completing the two hours. You'll hear that story just a little further on.

Now I had to complete my flying obligation. One day passed by. Then another day passed by. The fog was always there and flying was out of the question. All I needed was for the fog to do me the courtesy of lifting for just a couple of hours. Finally, on the third morning, the fog was gone. I ran to my airplane, loaded the only bag of sand in sight, put my barograph around my neck, and took off. I soon found myself flying in layers of peaceful clouds that you find only above 3,000 feet. Between the layers were apertures of beautiful blue sky. I entered one of the apertures and rose with wide turns. I flew higher and higher from one layer to the other. I felt like I was flying on a sea of cotton wool highlighted by magical reflections of pink and blue. I was so ecstatic at the beauty that I climbed at a shamefully slow pace. But I was always careful to keep my eye on the field beneath me through one of the apertures so that I could take action in case the clouds started to close.

Then, without warning, right in the middle of my exultation, my engine died. It was that old magneto playing tricks on me again. I had no choice but to go down. I descended carefully through the clouds, feeling their cold and the humidity. Finally, I got below the clouds and all I could think of was my uncompleted two hours. I sulked all through the landing. My friends scurried around me, the mechanics turned their attention to the magneto....and the fog returned.

I spent the next few days gritting my teeth in anger. Then, on January 27, 1916, the sun was shining as if it were almost spring and they sent me out again to do my two hours. I was told that I could go a little distance from the Busto Field but not stray too far. I flew straight for Malpensa, flew around that area for a while and then headed back to Busto. But all of a sudden I spotted beautiful Lake Maggiore in front of me. I had not seen it since qualifying for my First License. And there was my home town of Intra smack in the middle of the vista looking like a queen [see Figure 1]. Now I was in a quandary. Should I head for Intra or shouldn't I? On the one hand, there was the history of the magneto and the automatic feeding pump quitting on me. On the other hand, if I didn't go now, I would probably never go because after this flight, they would send me to the front. For whatever reason, flying over our own hometown was the most cherished ambition of all for the student pilots. Some pilots even faced house arrest, prison, and a suspension in flight pay to fly over their hometowns against orders. For most pilots the best opportunity to fly over their hometowns came during their final Raid. Notifying the townspeople in advance of their plans at the appropriate time, they took a little detour from their prescribed course and flew over their own countryside, above their own homes, enjoying the emotional highs of having their parents, family, and friends looking up at them with pride. They often even dropped a little written note down to them. Of the three pilots who came from Intra at that time, I would be the first to fly over the city. In fact, I would be the first person from Intra to ever fly a plane period. The temptation was too strong. I had to go for it.

I have never since experienced as intense emotion as I felt on that flight. As I approached Lake Maggiore, it became an increasing wonder to behold. From a distance it appeared no more than a decorative pendant suspended under the massive Alps mountains which rose up like a gathering of white giants around their leader, the Monte Rosa peak. But as I drew nearer, the lake turned into a huge blue carpet stretched out in welcome to the smaller hills. My wings were covered with hundreds of glittering ice cycles conspicuous against the blue of the sky. The rumble of the engine gave voice to the joy I felt. That gaiety of water, sky, and mountains from the emptiness of 6,000 feet made me wish that instead of that sack of sand there was a real person next to me to smile with.

I soared above my entire little world of beautiful small towns, lakes, islands, and mountains. On the one hand, they seemed so much less significant against the immensity of the blue sky. On the other hand, they seemed so intimate and solid because they symbolized Terra Firma. I passed over Intra at exactly twelve noon. I passed over the bell tower, the church, the roof of my house, and finally, when I passed over the cemetery where my loved ones were buried, I brought my hand up to salute them.

Needless to add, I kept an eye out for a place to land in case my engine failed again. Unfortunately, meadows which I had remembered as being very wide, didn't seem like such great candidates for a landing from several thousand feet up. Fortunately, the engine didn't fail and I finally headed back for the Busto Field. The two hours that I needed had passed and it was time to land. I throttled down the motor, made a beautiful single turn from 6,000 feet to the ground, and ended up with a picture book landing right in the middle of the field. The instructors were aware that I had strayed farther than I was supposed to but since everything went well, they didn't say anything about it. At last, I had officially earned my Second License and no one could take away that Crown from my Golden Eagles.

I thought of my family in Intra who might have guessed that it was me flying overhead and might be worried. I ran to the telephone, called my cousins in Intra who had a phone, and asked them to contact my family to let them know that I was safe and sound. That's when I found out that my family was at lunch when I was flying over their house and didn't even hear my plane. I guess I was flying high enough that the factory whistle, which always blew at noon, muffled the rumbling of my engine. My family was worried over my safety but were very happy to hear that the flight had gone well.

That night I went to Milano to have my Crown over the Golden Eagles admired because the population of Busto seemed too small an audience.

CONCLUSION

MY BIG FALL

On leaving the hospital after recovering from the mange, I reported immediately to the Headquarters of the Battalion Schools in Torino. The man in charge was a courageous Major who flew in spite of a very bad case of myopia that even heavy glasses could not fully correct. He risked his life every time he landed. When he visited an air field and invited one of the students to fly with him, the poor student was always scared to death. One foggy day, when the Major happened to be visiting Busto, we tried to avoid his asking any of the students to fly with him by telling him a little white lie – that is, that all of the students were already up in the air. I helped to convince him of the fact by boarding a plane and flying back and forth all around the field.

When I presented myself to this same Major in Torino , he looked at my orders and asked if I would volunteer to become a flying instructor. My answer was negative and he replied with "You will do as I say. By the way, you're wearing a red border around your Eagles. You're out of uniform, lieutenant." I got mad as hell because I had volunteered to become a pilot so that I could go to the front in a squadron. In fact, I was so mad that I actually considered asking to be relieved of my obligations because of neurasthenia.

The following morning, though, I got a real surprise. I was told that the Major had selected me to transport planes from the Taliedo Air Field near Milano to the squadrons in Verona - about 100 miles due east - in expectation that a place would soon be available in the squadrons for me. "Long Live Italy!". A sergeant was to help me transport the planes after we made a few test flights with them around the Taliedo Field. I got hold of the sergeant and, together, we caught the first train to Milano and then onto Taliedo. By the time we got there it was already dark. The next morning, we were given two new planes. The sergeant looked over his plane and I looked over mine. I tried to start the engine but it wouldn't start. By the time the engine was fixed and I was ready to take off, it was already evening again. Barely off the ground, I noticed that the altimeter didn't work. I came down, got another altimeter, and took off again. I was at an altitude of about 6,000 feet. It was the 8th of February, there was a light fog, and, for some reason, the flight felt very sad. It was the first time that I had flown over a large city. The gray roofs, the gray houses, the gray sky, and the approaching nightfall made me feel sad as I had never felt before. A premonition perhaps?

Impulsively, I was in a hurry to bring the plane down and catch the train to Milano. I began my glide and noticed that the train which went back and forth between Milano and Taliedo every half hour was about to pull into the Taliedo train station. If I didn't hurry, I would miss catching that train back to Milano. I landed at the end of the field and tore off for the hangers at great speed. To pick up more speed, I lifted the tail end of the plane. Too much as it turned out. Suddenly, before I had a chance to turn off the engine, CRASH! The plane nosed down. I was thrown forward and found myself on the ground near the plane, which had turned upside down. I could hear that the engine was still rumbling. I tried to get up and get away before the gasoline, that I assumed was by now leaking out of the tank, caught fire. But I couldn't move. One of my legs was broken. For a split second, I expected to die in flames. Then, thank God, the engine died and there was silence. Luckily, the gas tanks were new and had not broken. Unluckily, the leather seat belt, which was also new, had broken. If it hadn't I might have come out of it with only a few pulled stomach muscles. On the other hand I could just as easily have been burned alive or smashed under a detached engine. All things considered, I was happy with my broken leg.

The ambulance arrived and brought me to the hospital. There they found that I was suffering from a comminuted fracture to the tibia of the right leg. To put it simply, my leg was shattered. If it weren't for the fact that I was wearing leather leggings reinforced with a thin sheet of steel exactly where my leg was hit – normally I wore soft ones – the damage would have been even more severe and the leg would have had to be amputated.

I never recovered from the injury. The bone was shattered and some of its fragments remained permanently in the flesh and eventually rotted. Every once in a while, both during and after the war, I would need a scraping operation. I spent the remainder of the war partly in bed and partly on crutches. But my real pain was not to have flown over enemy territory even once. All that training and all that effort had been rendered futile. I had maimed myself for nothing on the very first flight after receiving my Second License. I console myself by thinking that if I had broken my leg on the previous flight, I would never have received my Second License.

My friends went to the squadrons. Many died, but they died for something. Some returned with silver medals for bravery. One even got a gold medal. A cousin of mine, Lieutenant Eduardo Scavini, who was with me in the course for the First License at Malpensa, returned with three silver medals. Unfortunately he died of typhoid after the war. I am including one of his letters as an example of what it was like to fly in the front, where I would never go.

FLIGHT OF WAR

Aviano Military Aviation Field
March 6, 1916

My Dearest Mama,

Thank you so much for your recent letter and for all the good news. This past week I have been very busy preparing for my many bombing flights. I have also been troubled by a case of conjunctivitis which I caught during a flight in which I was in the middle of a storm without my glasses. Now my eyes are feeling better though. On Sunday I went with another five Caproni planes to bomb Adelsberg in Austria [see Figure 1]. I picked up a fair amount of artillery fire and was happy to get back to the field.

Yesterday we tried to execute another raid but a huge, thick barrier of clouds stopped us from crossing our own borders. Last night the order came for two Capronis to conduct a follow-up raid on Adelsberg. I was to go on one of them.

At seven this morning, we left the Aviano Field and went directly toward the sea. Just as we were entering Isonzo, the other plane suddenly turned back because of engine trouble. I continued alone on my route over the sea, admiring the beauty of the Gulf of Trieste and the Istria Peninsula. Underneath me, four torpedo boats followed on the sea in case I was forced to land over water. I entered into enemy territory leaving Trieste way off to my left and arrived without a problem in the vicinity of Adelsberg.

I was almost directly over the city and aimed my telescopic site at the train station. All of a sudden, the whistling sounds started. I pulled the trigger releasing the first bombs at the station. I looked around. For a moment, I was in a daze. I was being surrounded by bursts of projectiles. They were like hundreds of confetti being hurled at me. I could see long tracks of them coming from many locations on the ground and aiming at my plane. With every burst, my plane made a sudden jump.

The sergeant alongside me pointed to several bullet holes in the wings and was gesturing to me as if to say, "what are we going to do?" I still had two bombs left. By this time we had passed over Adelsberg, so I made a 180 degree turn to return and finish the job. The artillery fire was intensifying and the projectiles were coming closer and closer to my plane. It felt as if the projectiles were being hurled at me by thousands of angry men for the sole purpose of seeing me crash. But for some reason, instead of fear, I felt something else. Something more noble. I felt a sense of duty requiring that I keep my wits about me. It was a personal satisfaction more rewarding than any other I have ever experienced.

Suddenly, one of the projectiles struck my plane with a very loud explosion. The gas tank had been hit. Now the odor of gunfire was intermingled with the odor of gasoline which gushed out of the tank in a strong jet and began wetting everything including us. The cockpit was getting filled with gasoline. The pressure in the tank was quickly decreasing and the engine began to sputter.

I looked in the direction of Italy and saw the sea very far below me and very far away. For just a moment, I felt that I might never see my homeland again. But the three of us on the plane seemed to form a communal silent pact of self preservation. And while the other two frantically hand pumped the gasoline without stopping, I guided the plane toward the sea. All the while, I tried to get rid of some of the gasoline in the cockpit by rolling the plane from side to side. The gunfire continued to pursue us and constantly made the plane jump and swerve. From a height of 9,000 feet, we saw the sea approaching us slowly —too slowly. Far out on the sea, we saw four black dots. They were the four torpedo boats awaiting our return. The prospect of joining our fellow countrymen was still a little doubtful to us, but the hope intensified our labor.

The other two men continued to hand pump the gasoline for a full half hour. Only during the brief periods of time when the two men switched places did the engine sputter even a little. The shoreline was nearing and beneath us appeared Trieste in a blaze of magnificent light. By now we felt certain we would reach Italy. We cut off the gas tank with holes in it which by that time had leaked more than 50 gallons of gasoline into the plane. When we did that, the left propeller stopped. From then on we only had two functioning engines and we had to use the rudder to control the direction of the plane.

We were at an altitude of about 8,400 feet when we noticed a small enemy fighter plane approaching us from the front. It was a Fokker. I immediately aimed at it with my forward machine gun while one of the other men stayed on alert at the rear machine gun waiting for the attack. We were ready for the battle. The plane passed me laterally at a distance of about 900 feet. I held it under fire with my machine gun until it disappeared behind my wing. Then it swung around and started attacking us from the back from a distance of about 300 feet. We kept shooting at it until we saw the Fokker stagger. It had been hit and it was soon out of sight.

By now we were over the sea. Our Caproni, missing one engine, was slowly losing altitude. I did my best to keep the plane up and pointing toward Grado. By the time we approached the Aviano Field, our altitude was only 60 feet. The other Caproni bomber, which had turned back at Isonzo because of engine trouble, had already been repaired and was on its way again to Adelsberg. Later, that plane also returned all full of holes. The pilots of that plane, who had been on bombing missions to several other cities, told me that they had never encountered any place as well armed with anti-aircraft fire as Adelsberg. And it had all been accomplished by the Austrians in the four days since we had begun our bombing missions against the city. That shows you how important it was to them. The whole thing was a harrowing experience but I'm proud to say that I didn't lose my head or think of the danger for a minute.

As always, I send my good wishes. I hope Aunt Ada gets well soon and that the rest of you are all in good health. Please give an affectionate kiss for me to Papa, Maria, Vittore, Grandmother, and all the aunts and uncles. And to you, a very tender embrace from your affectionate Edoardo.

DID I EVER FLY AGAIN?

Did I fly again after the big fall? Yes, but not for another four months. For four months, I lay in bed with my leg all bandaged up. They also suspended a weight on my leg that was supposed to prevent it from shrinking. My tibia and fibia bones had been smashed to bits and the nerves damaged. The little bone splinters finally fused sufficiently for me to walk on crutches.

But I could not get my mind off flying. Finally, I persuaded them to drive me to the Taliedo Field and I managed to drag myself to a Farman that was ready to fly. Naturally, I couldn't pilot myself. I had to be satisfied to be the passenger. At least, I was pleased to find that I still wasn't afraid to fly. I did feel a little fear when we landed but I decided that I would have been afraid to land with someone else doing the piloting even if I hadn't crashed.

I did, however, experience a very real fear of flying several months later. And probably with very good reason. While I was recovering from an operation to join some of the bone splinters, I ran into a friend I've already talked about who went to school with me at Malpensa. For quite some time his luck had held. St. Elia had saved him when he lost the ailerons on both his wings and miraculously fell to the ground without getting hurt. Then after he got his Second License, he went to a squadron and participated in a number of bombing missions. But the odds finally caught up with him. On his last mission, his co-pilot was killed and he seriously wounded. For his bravery he received a gold medal and we ended up in the same hospital.

My friend was barely strong enough when they sent him to Milano with some other men to prepare for the famous flight over Cattaro with D'Annunzio. I volunteered to join him on one of his test flights without realizing it was his first since the bombing mission in which he had been hurt and his friend had been killed. So it was that I found myself sitting next to him when he motioned to one of the mechanics to join us also. The mechanic turned white as a ghost and I immediately grasped the reason. The mechanic was scared to death that the pilot's lack of confidence would result in a tragedy for all of us. Oh poor me. But now how could I get off the plane? I certainly didn't want my friend to think that I was scared of flying with him because that would only make things worse. I stayed and hoped for the best. The mechanic boarded the plane still looking very pale, sat behind us in the middle of the three engines, and my friend took off. We climbed without a hitch to about 15,000 feet and leveled off. My friend made a few beautiful turns – not too timidly and not to recklessly – and then prepared to land. So far so good. When he straightened the plane to begin his glide, I gripped the bottom of my seat with both hands. We were "long" and would end up in the hangars sure as hell. I dared not look at my friend's face for fear of disturbing his concentration. Thank God, just in time, he throttled down, made a 180 degree turn, and went back to the end of the field to begin his glide again. This time, he was right on target. As the plane touched the ground, I heard him saying a Hail Mary. The wheels touched the ground with a kiss and the poor mechanic deplaned with a sigh of relief. I too was never so happy to step on terra firma.

I flew a third time, also as a passenger, on a Caproni with Lieutenant Campioni as the pilot. On that flight he made the first *loops* ever conducted by that model. Sadly, Campioni was later killed during take off.

The fourth and final time I flew didn't go very well. A wounded Colonel who was at the hospital with me wanted to fly so we went together to the Taliedo Field. We had at our disposal a Caproni 600HP. The Colonel sat at the bow of the cockpit, the two pilots sat behind him, and I started to sit on a little seat over the wings that was normally occupied by the machine gunner. They decided that I shouldn't sit in that exposed position to avoid the possibility of a mishap injuring my other leg. So they asked me to stand between the two gasoline tanks without realizing that

I could only stand on one leg and before I could object, they took off.

Everything was fine up to 9,000 feet. Then one of the two pilots - excuse me for calling him the stupider one - decided to entertain the Colonel by making loops. We were over the Central Station of Milano. One minute the tracks of the station were on my right and the next minute they were on my left, then they were above me and then they were under me. My body slammed against the end of the airplane and I was almost hurled out. What a horrible experience that was. All I could do was to hang onto the rims of the gas tanks with all the strength I had and pray once more to St. Elia for the idiot to stop.

Finally he did. I refrained from punching his face partly out of respect for the Colonel and partly because I lacked the strength. I was so mad that I couldn't even speak to him after we landed. It wouldn't have done any good anyway. Besides, he was a Captain and I was a Lieutenant. And if that wasn't bad enough, later I had to endure his boasting of the loops he had performed to impress the Colonel.

After that I never flew again. At times I wanted to, but for some reason, I just couldn't bring myself to do it. Hopefully, I will fly again when my son grows up and I can teach him how to fly. Planes will be so advanced by that time that it should be very easy to learn. Only God understands what joy that will give me.

Now let me tell you some of the fantasies that I have had since my flying days. I believe they are fantasies that will become realities. But just in case they don't, take them with a grain of salt.

PART II: REFLECTIONS 20 YEARS LATER

FOREWORD

After his tragic accident in 1916, Viglino went on to obtain degrees in Law, Literature, and Philosophy, and became a professor at the Collegio Mellerio Rosmini in Domodossola, where he had studied as a youth. He became a prolific writer, authoring numerous articles on religious subjects, personal experiences, and childrens' school texts. Finally, he became the Editor of the Rivista Rosminiana , a Catholic newspaper published in Intra.

In 1930, he married Ida Ferraris. Their first child, Vittorio was born in 1931. In 1934, Viglino appended his memoirs with a number of surprisingly intuitive reflections on the future of aviation, the automobile, space travel, and other inventions of the 20th century. They demonstrate both his foresight and the tenor of the times.

Sadly, after having survived his daredevil exploits in aviation, Viglino succumbed to pneumonia and died in 1935 at the early age of forty-three.

AVIATION

In my opinion, the plane will completely change the world. How? It will reduce the distance between countries in the same way that the railroad has reduced the distance between cities and regions within a country. Indeed, I believe the time will come when planes will fly throughout the world as frequently and as reliably as trains do today. And when that happens, man will travel from one end of the earth to the other as readily as he travels from one end of the city to the other by trolley today. Just compare our travels today to those of our grandparents. We travel more miles in a year—and often in a month or a week—than they did in their entire lifetimes. Is there any reason to think that this progression will stop?

How will man benefit from all the easy and frequent air travel? By becoming more homogeneous through increased contact with his fellow man from all parts of the world. This has already begun to take place in America where Italians, French, Germans, etc. mingle and intermarry. People will no longer feel bound to remain in their native homeland; they will settle wherever they prosper best. Do you really think that the Chinese will stay in China if they can earn a better living in Italy or in America? As people become familiar with the customs, languages, and viewpoints of those who live in different countries, national boundaries will disappear and there will emerge a more unified, more civilized, more tolerant society. I predict that within fifty years after the plane has fully established the ease and frequency of travel I've described, there will have emerged a single nation, a single race, and a single language. And war will have forever disappeared.

* * *

As I see it, aviation technology is currently heading down four different paths:

    (1) Further development of existing technology. One example in this category is the German hydroplane "Do

X". It has a single huge wing and twelve 500HP engines. Descending, it skims across the surface of the water, settles down, and then functions like a boat. It can comfortably carry 100 people and has already flown almost half way across the Atlantic. With more powerful engines it might be possible for it to have a wing span and body large enough to carry 3,000 or 4,000 people just like the ocean liners.

A second example of such planes is a bomber built by our own Engineer Caproni. It achieves 6000HP, can carry 18,000 lb of explosives, 33,000 lb of fuel, and travels up to 126 mph.

A third example is the gigantic 2400HP German "Junker" which even carries passengers in the wings.

(2) The Helicopter. The Spaniard La Cierva has built this plane which I described earlier. When I saw it fly in Rome, I just stood there with my mouth open. It's an ingenious invention. When it's perfected, this plane will be able to land and take off from your own patio. For sure, it beats all the rest of them for safety.

(3) The Jet Plane. In theory, this plane is extremely simple. It has no traditional engine or propeller. The forward motion of the plane is achieved by what are, in effect, a series of explosions in the back of the plane. The backward thrust of the explosions create an equal and opposite force propelling the plane forward. The designer has flown for several miles in the new plane and is now in the process of perfecting it. If this method of propulsion catches on and sufficient explosive power is used, a speed of 1,200 or 1,800 mph could be achieved within the next 20 to 40 years. Whereas some people will be able to tolerate the intense noise of the jet, others will be uncomfortable until the plane goes faster than the speed of sound.

At a speed of 1,200 mph, it would take about 3 hours to fly across the Atlantic. With the time difference of about 5 hours, if we left Milano at 7:00 am we would arrive in New York at 5:00 am, just in time to have coffee. Of course, we would lose the 2 hours on our return. Actually, I fully expect the day to come when a transatlantic journey will take no more than a half hour. And those reading my book at that time will be amused by how conservative my predictions were.

(4) The Personal Vehicle. Imagine an extraordinarily small plane that flies at 75 mph with a single 8HP engine. It consists of a single wing having no fuselage, tail, or carriage. Such a plane has already flown magnificently and proved extremely stable. If it catches on, everyone will be able to own and fly his own plane. Instead of the 30,000 liras which a plane costs today, it would cost only 10,000—about the price of a car. It could be that this plane, with its very modest horsepower requirement, could actually transport more passengers per HP than the "Dos X".

Only God knows which of these four paths will enjoy the greatest success. Personally, I am intrigued by the small 8HP plane probably because I love to fly myself and will always dream of having my own plane. On the other hand, the helicopter, with its greater assurance that I won't break my one good leg, also has its attractions.

*** * ***

We have already begun to reach heights of 48,000 to 60,000 feet with balloons. I think it likely that passenger planes will also attain these altitudes in transatlantic flights. And when they do, it will be possible for them to travel at much greater speeds. In fact, in Germany they are currently developing a plane that will travel at 600 mph at an altitude of 45,000 feet. Once perfected, such a plane could fly to America in about 6 hours—about the time it takes to go from Milano to Firenze by train.

* * *

Significant developments are already occurring in the area of space travel. Just recently, in Germany, a manned rocket reached a height of 30,000 feet in about one minute. It then took ten minutes for the man inside to parachute back to earth. Two Frenchmen have funded a yearly prize of 5,000 francs for the best work in astrophysics. They envision a passenger carrying rocket propelled by subatomic energy going to the moon. Indeed, within a few generations, everyone will have the opportunity to go to the moon. Let's just hope that England and France don't manage to colonize the moon just as effectively as they have managed to colonize so much of the earth.

Once we start traveling in outer space, we'll have to make some changes in our manner of speaking. For one thing, we'll need to refrain from using the word "lunatic" so as to not offend the inhabitants of the moon. And referring to someone as "departed from this earth" could simply mean that the person has embarked on a journey in space.

THE AUTOMOBILE

The advent of advanced aviation will not diminish the role of the automobile. But I don't believe that the car will keep running on gasoline. Cars of the future will run on electric power but not from batteries. Marconi has already rung the first death bell for the internal combustion engine by sending a small amount of electric power from Genoa over a distance of about 10,000 miles to turn on the lights at the Sydney Exposition. Power plants all over the world will distribute exactly the required amount of electric power to every motor in the world via radio transmission. Each motor will contain a registered meter indicating the amount of energy consumed. At the end of each month the meter will be read and the appropriate charge will be made for the power. The charge could be made by a single world-wide federation whose function is to govern the production and distribution of power. However, if it becomes difficult for the world wide federation to account for all the power utilized – for example, how do you hunt down a guy in Tibet who is using power but not paying for it – then each country could be assigned its own unique wavelength and the meters in that country would be limited to their assigned frequency.

And it won't be just cars running on electronic transmission. All motors will. Kitchen appliances, hot water heaters, furnaces, planes, trains, etc. God help us though when this energy, for whatever reason, comes to a screeching halt. The world will stop functioning in the same way that the whole city stops functioning today when trains don't run.

Hopefully, once cars are running on electric engines, the deafening noise and the air pollution that they create will be eliminated. And what a blessing that will be. I hear they've chemically analyzed 9 cubic feet of air from a busy street in downtown Paris and found that 50% of it was automobile exhaust. I'm convinced that the rise in the incidence of tuberculosis is caused by pollution. But maybe the next generation will adjust to the automobile and become more robust as a result. I hear that in America, where they have a car for every four inhabitants (at least before the depression), people actually have a stronger constitution than we do.

Even I will buy the electric car of the future. But I sure wouldn't buy the car of today. To drive it requires seven senses and I only have five. With your hands you have to control the steering wheel, the stick shift, and the hand brake. With your feet you have to control the accelerator, the clutch, and the brake. With your eyes you have to see everything around you including the road behind. And with all this going on, you have to make a thousand judgments to successfully pass another car, avoid running over the curb, avoid hitting another car, avoid another car hitting you, avoid hitting a pedestrian, etc. It's too much work. Thankfully, the electric car will go at a slower speed and will have a shorter range thus making it a lot easier and more fun to drive. And you will be less likely to kill yourself. With one or two buttons on the steering wheel, you'll be able to control everything. Hopefully too the streets will be emptied of the speed loving mafia members who will be too bored with the slow moving electric cars. And that will be the day when horses will finally disappear. They will end up in the museum, objects of curiosity for our grandchildren to stare at.

RADIO AND TELEVISION

"To hell with the radio and all who spend all their time listening to it" my mother says. And she's not altogether wrong. Even my brother, Carlo, seems to be suffering from a bad case of radio-mania and he's got plenty of company. He bought a radio a few years ago but at first it didn't work and he couldn't figure out why. Then he moved it into a different room and, unfortunately, the radio suddenly started working. He's become completely addicted to it. None of us would object if he listened to it 5 or 10 minutes a day. Although the noise is a nuisance, it is bearable for short periods of time. But Carlo spends every minute that he's not working glued to the radio. He comes home from the office at noon, stays at the table for just the few minutes it takes him to eat, then runs to the radio until 2:00. In the evening, it's the same thing. After dinner, he turns on the radio from 7:00 to 11:00 for his night time orgy. I dread to think what would happen if Carlo didn't have to work. At times I fear he has become brain dead for he thinks and talks about nothing else. Hopefully once the novelty is gone and he realizes that the voice coming from Vienna or London has no more importance than the one coming from nearby Cavoretto, he'll become bored. But that may be too optimistic. More likely, his addiction to the radio is incurable. The maid says that if she could afford it, she would destroy the damn thing.

What's down the road? Television will permit the transmission of images as well as sound. Just recently, I saw a combination radio/television performance from New York. Even though the actors were miles away, you felt like you were watching a theater performance except that the images of the actors on the screen were too flat. I think that in the future, the images will be projected full sized and three dimensional [holography]. That's when we'll be able to attend every performance in the world from our own homes: operas and symphonies from Paris and Turin, Papal appearances from Rome, and boxing matches from America.

Who knows? Unlike my household, perhaps the ability to attend the many musical and dramatic performances, sports, etc. on radio/television from the home will be beneficial to family unity. It may be too much to wish for but it might also help the young by keeping them away from coffee houses and bars. More importantly, radio/television may allow students to attend school from at home. Miscreants who deserve a good slap will get one from their teacher's image, although I'm not sure that it will have any effect on them in this veritable mad house of the future.

In addition to television, I think phono-vision will come in strong and have a huge unifying impact on our society. The day will come when instead of carrying a watch in our vest pocket, we will carry a little gadget to transmit sound and images. It will be about the size of a pocket watch but instead of a clock face it will have a lens to transmit the images. With it we will be able to dial the numbers of our friends who have the same gadget and, not only communicate with them, but see their faces in the lens. In fact, the image of your friend will be projected full scale in three dimensions right next to you. Think of what a nice option that will be if your friend happens to be one of those with the bad habit of shaking your hand too hard, or stepping on your feet by coming too close to you.

THE PHONOGRAPH

There were several years just after the war when it looked like the phonograph would soon be a goner. It continued to be used in the inns and taverns of small mountain towns but in the large cities it was much less popular. I and the better part of mankind heaved a sigh of relief. The reason for its expected demise was that it improved very little. Granted, it did become a little more practical because the large metal cylinders containing the sound were replaced by much smaller disks. But it still continued to produce singing, playing and talking with almost as much scratching as in the early days. The first time I heard a phonograph, I was 5 years old and sick in bed. My parents bought the phonograph as a reward for my taking my medicine. When I first heard the sounds from it, I got scared half to death. I thought they were coming straight from hell (We were one of the few people that had a phonograph in their homes. I remember my father asking my mother to please stop making any noise, including playing the piano, while he was listening to the phonograph because he didn't want any other sounds to detract from his enjoyment of the music. Then he would end up in his study, which was several rooms away from where the phonograph was playing. Maybe he was just looking for an excuse to stop her from playing the piano).

But more recently things have turned around. Today the phonograph is even more popular than it was when it first appeared and I feel sure that it will continue to live. It has undergone some important improvements. To begin with, the scratching has been greatly reduced. I recently passed by an open window from which singing was coming and I couldn't tell if the singing was from a woman or from a phonograph. They've also perfected its construction and made it much smaller in size. I once had the misfortune of living in a rooming house for several years with neighbors on either side of me both ardent phonograph lovers. They played their phonograph from 7:00 in the morning until 10:00 at night. And I was trying to write. You can imagine how much fun that was. So I got as much sleep as I could during the day and wrote from 10:00 at night until 7:00 in the morning.

One improvement that has come about just in the last year and probably guarantees the phonograph at least another fifty years of life is the technology used for storing sound. It amounts to storing the sound molecularly on a metal wire. The metal wire eliminates the scratching altogether and is capable of storing a lot more sound than the disk. In fact, if the new technology had been available back when I was rooming between the two noisy nuisances, I could have gotten even with them by playing the wire player all day long at peak volume and then left the house. What a marvelous application for the new invention.

I've heard that the metal wire technology has been used to store the reading of the entire Bible by a prominent actor. How I would love to listen to Dante's Divine Comedy read by someone like Pastonchi who has the talent to bring out the subtleties which escape you when you're reading the book yourself. With time, all of the wonderful classics will be available via this technology.

And it looks like there are even are better things to come than the phonograph. There's a new gadget called the *dictaphone* that can make writing obsolete. Now there is no longer any need to write anything. You just speak into the dictaphone, the typist puts it on paper and you sign it. Or you can even send the metal wire storing what you said directly to the recipient and he just plays it on his dictaphone. I'm not looking forward to the time when the dictaphone makes it so easy for man to create so many words that people won't have the incentive to write anymore. Writing tends to keep down the number of words because the number of people that can write is smaller than the number of people that can talk. And besides, writing, either with a pen or a typewriter, makes your hands tired.

At this point, I'd better stop. There's no use scaring ourselves thinking about a tragedy that hasn't yet occurred.

Just be happy that I had to write these observations. If I had dictated them, they would have been much longer.

THE BICYCLE

The bicycle has not changed significantly in thirty years. And now that we've developed gearshift systems to facilitate changes in speed, I suppose the basic bicycle will remain the same forever. Aside from minor improvements in the brakes or in the gears, it can no more improved than the wagon or the umbrella. And so it goes that on the seventh day God rested.

Wouldn't it be wonderful though if we could put wings and a propeller on the bicycle and go cycling up in the sky on our aviocycle. Then we would be able to enjoy the full view of the sky and the earth like we used to with the old planes of my time. What fun it would be to supply the horsepower with your own legs. Imagine that you start cycling upwards. You see a little cloud just above you. You start peddling toward it. Pedal, pedal and you start climbing. Higher, higher, and you're in the clouds. No, you went a little too far. The little cloud you were aiming for is just below you. Pedal down a little, a free-form glide, and there you are. A dense patch of clouds blows across your face. You can't see anything. The clattering of the gears becomes louder. You're completely immersed in fog. You're cold and a little afraid because you're disoriented. You peddle downhill to escape from the clouds. You're out. You're safe. Now you just peddle along enjoying the blue sky and the bright sun above you.

Suddenly, you spot another aviocycle coming towards you. Is it him or not? Yes, it's your good friend Gigino who falls in alongside you. Without the noise of a motor, the two of you chit chat happily with a cigarette in your mouth. All of a sudden Gigino disappears. He's gone to take a little dive in the clouds. You decide not to follow him because with the poor visibility, if he makes a sudden turn, you could collide. Look, he reappears right in front of you. The two of you decide to race. Off you go!

Pretty soon it's time to go home. You turn around and coast downward in a wide arc. The only thing you have to worry about is going so fast that your wings break off. But you have your speedometer on the handlebars. Now you're about 300 feet from land. You straighten out and start peddling again. A damned air train creates turbulence and makes the ride a little bumpy for both of you. The air currents from the tiles of the roofs of the houses add to the bumpiness just as you are about to land. Finally, you head straight down, make a half turn, and your wheels touch down on the town air plaza.

AFTERWORD

I have an old house in the country. It's in a little town near Intra on top of a hill. Completely isolated from civilization and the world. There are no modern conveniences. No motor bus. Just a horse drawn carriage. No drinking water on tap because the town is so high. No stores. The residents all shop in another little town nearby. No gas for cooking. They've had electric lights for only a few years. Very few people live in the town—the parish priest, the doctor, the teacher. You're lucky to find someone to exchange a few words with. You have to walk three miles just to get to the nearest railroad station. You couldn't possibly raise a family there. You would have to send your children to another town to attend grade school.

It's quite possible that twenty years from now, or maybe even sooner, you'll be able to live in a country house like mine and work in a large city like Torino. With planes flying at 1,000 miles per hour, you'll be able to reach several large cities from your country home with just a half hour flight. Or perhaps you'll fly a plane to and from work just like people living in the suburbs now take an automobile or a bus. You'll be able to shop for your groceries and such in the city and bring them home with you. Or you may elect to have your purchases flown to your house on a plane owned by the store or a delivery service. When it's cold, you'll be able to fly to the warmth of Palermo, Sicily. When it's hot, you'll be able to fly to the cool temperature of Berlin, Germany. For entertainment, you'll be able to enjoy spectacles from all over the world via television. And you'll never get lonely because you'll be able to talk to and see your friends via the phono-vision gadget in your vest pocket.

But to tell the truth, I personally am not looking forward to any of these things. For me, they threaten the solitude and peace and quiet that I so much enjoy in that old house in the country. Tell me, what solitude will there be when your ears and eyes and brain are constantly bombarded by noise and pictures from all the electronic devices. When you can be reached within a half hour by plane from 500 miles away. When the poles are crowded with people visiting during their summer season. When Central Africa is crowded with people visiting during their winter season. When the entire earth is as bustling with people as our city streets are today. There will be no place on earth where you can be alone. When you try to find refuge on top of the Himalayas, you'll find that there's a Himalaia-Kulm Hotel there. No place will be peaceful. Not the earth, filled with people. Not the sky, filled with planes. When that time comes, death will no longer be our eternal rest. It will be our only rest.

For all my ramblings about the radio, the motorcycle, the automobile, and the other contraptions that already have been or will be invented, I don't believe for a minute that they are the most important things in life. They don't nourish the soul. They are toys. Marvelous toys, yes. But still toys. They're means to an end, not ends in themselves. They are here to serve us, not to be served by us. When I see people listening to music on the radio for hours on end, I can't help but notice that they're not really enjoying the music. They're enjoying the machine that makes the music. And when I see people going for a ride on a motorcycle, an automobile, or an airplane, I can't help but notice that they're not enjoying the scenery afforded by the ride. They're enjoying the speed of the machine. I've seen people who have never stayed for a Sunday morning sermon listen attentively to one coming over the radio. Even Christianity has become mechanized. If Jesus Christ returned to earth he would have to deliver his sermons over the radio or no one would listen to him. The products of mother nature don't appeal to anyone anymore. To get our attention, everything has to come through a machine. If it can't be mechanized, it has no value.

My fear is that new inventions will never come to an end. And if they don't, goodbye to the enjoyment of nature, the tranquility of the human spirit, the value of humanity. Actually, I'm content just to carry a little watch in my vest pocket. And I regret not having been around at the time when even that wasn't available.

I just hope that my simple house in the country remains the peaceful refuge that it is today, if not until the end of all time, at least until the end of my time.

ISBN 155212933-0